Texas Law
of
Streets and Alleys

A Handbook

Kenneth L Bennight Jr

ISBN: 1937345629
ISBN-13: 9781937345624

Acknowledgments:

I owe a debt to many people in preparing this handbook. I could not have written this without the knowledge and collegiality of the lawyers in the San Antonio City Attorney's Office. The help I got in critique sessions at the San Antonio Writers' Guild was invaluable. And, of course, the time I devoted to this required the tolerance of my wife of 44 years, Susan.

My most unusual debt of gratitude is to a man I never met. Jackson Hubbard was a San Antonio Deputy City Attorney before I joined the City Attorney's Office, and he left behind two memos discussing some of the materials addressed here. It was those memos that gave me the boost I needed to understand the peculiarities of street law.

Kenneth Bennight

This is the only place in the world where the pavements consist exclusively of holes with asphalt around them. And they are the most economical in the world, because holes never get out of repair.

Mark Twain

What You Need to Know About Texas Street Law

1. Why Should I Read This?

Few lawyers and fewer non-lawyers give much thought to the legal rights and obligations associated with streets. To most people, streets are just something you drive on. Street law does not approach the complexity of the securities laws or the Internal Revenue Code, but it does involve applying ordinary real estate principles in seemingly arcane contexts. This handbook's goals are to help real estate professionals and those in city government think through the legal implications of street-related problems and to suggest beneficial outcomes in areas of possible disagreement.

This is written primarily for lawyers, paralegals, and other real estate professionals. The subject matter requires use of real estate terms such as "easement" and "fee." Most in the target audience will know these terms. If you do not, an Internet search will quickly lead you to definitions.

Briefly, an **easement** is a right to use someone else's property for a specific purpose. **Fee simple absolute** is the type of ownership we are all familiar with. Saying that you own land is usually an informal way of saying you hold the fee-simple interest in the land. There are other types of fees besides fee simple absolute, *e.g.*, fee simple determinable, fee on a condition subsequent, and fee for a term of years. You need not understand these terms to understand what is said here.

This handbook will use the term "fee" in place of "fee simple absolute" to minimize turgidity, and because the rights and obligations of the fee owner will generally apply to the holder of any type of fee interest, simple or otherwise.

This handbook refers to cities, and the principles discussed apply to them. But most of the same principles apply as well to counties and county roads. As such, this handbook may be useful to county attorneys as well as city attorneys.

---

2. Who Owns the Streets?

2.01. General Principles.

If you advise a city or county on street-related issues, you will be asked about street ownership, probably regularly. Replying that the city or county owns the streets misleads your questioner. Try to find out why the client is asking, in part because a client asking that question is likely making his own legal analysis. Get to the underlying issue so you can provide your own legal analysis.

First, the State of Texas owns all public street easements,[1] while cities manage and control streets within their corporate boundaries[2] as counties do for roads outside any corporate limits.[3] The Texas Department of Transportation maintains state and federal highways.[4] See Section 10 (TxDOT Turnback Program). State ownership of public street easements is how, for example, formerly

---

[1] *West v. City of Waco*, 294 S.W. 832, 833–34 (Tex. 1927).

[2] Tex. Transp. Code Ann. §§ 311.001–.004 (West 2013).

[3] *Id.* § 251.004.

[4] *Texas Dep't of Transp. v. City of Sunset Valley*, 146 S.W.3d 637, 644 (Tex. 2004).

county roads automatically become city streets when an area is newly annexed.[5] No compensation for loss of the roads is due to the county, because the county did not own them. It just managed and controlled them. Counties are usually happy enough that the city assumes the maintenance obligation.

State ownership played an important role in *Texas Department of Transportation v. City of Sunset Valley*.[6] Sunset Valley is a small suburb in the southern part of Austin. In the course of improving U.S. 290, TxDOT closed a portion of Jones Road, an important connecting street. As it happens, Sunset Valley had acquired the Jones Road right-of-way in fee and used that ownership as one basis for its claim for compensation. But the Texas Supreme Court stated that, though title was in the name of Sunset Valley, Sunset Valley held that title for the benefit of the state and the public. Sunset Valley was not entitled to compensation, because cities have no proprietary rights or rights of exclusive possession in streets. Instead, cities hold streets in trust for the state and for the public.[7] To emphasize, even though Sunset Valley took fee title in its own name, title to the street right-of-way interest was really in the state.

The *Sunset Valley* case aside, state ownership is only rarely germane to resolving a problem. And saying that the state owns the streets begs the underlying question of the nature of the ownership, *i.e.*, does the state own the fee or an easement? Whether

---

[5] Tex. Loc. Gov't Code Ann. § 43.056(b)(6) (West Supp. 2013).

[6] 146 S.W.3d 637 (Tex. 2004).

[7] *Id.* at 644–45.

the street is fee or easement is most often what the client needs
to know.

To distinguish between fee streets and easement streets, you have
to know how the particular street came to be. The principal ways
streets come to be are:

   a. *Recorded Plats.* The vast majority of streets exist because
   they are laid out by recorded plat.

   b. *Historical Paths.* Some streets derive from historical paths
   of travel that arose before anyone thought of ownership.
   San Antonio has an unusual twist on this category. See
   Section 2.04 (San Antonio's Historical Streets).

   c. *Widened and Rerouted Streets.* Some streets would be in
   one of the two categories above, but they have been widened or rerouted in ways that may alter their character.

2.02. Platted Streets.

2.02.01. The General Rule.

Most of the streets we drive on were created by subdivision plat.
That includes connector and arterial streets as well as residential ones. Unless the plat provides otherwise, a platted street is a
public street right-of-way easement.[8] Plats should never provide

---

[8] *Eidelbach v. Davis*, 99 S.W.2d 1067, 1072 (Tex. Civ. App.—Beaumont 1936, writ
dism'd): *Texas Co. v. Texarkana Mach. Shops*, 1 S.W.2d 928, 931 (Tex. Civ. App.—
Texarkana 1928, no writ); *cf, Preston v. City of Navasota*, 34 Tex. 684 (1870).

otherwise. A city that permits plats to create fee interests in rights-of-way (whether street, drainage, or something else) is creating unnecessary problems for itself.

Ownership of the fee under platted street easements remains with the owner of the abutting property, except in unusual circumstances. When different people own different sides of an easement street, they each own the fee to the centerline. This is so even though most real estate transactions use property descriptions that do not include the street right-of-way. Even in those transactions, ownership of the fee under the street passes to the grantee as an appurtenance to an abutting parcel or by means of the strip-and-gore doctrine.[9] For emphasis, even if a deed conveys by lot and block number and even if the plat shows the street as separate from the lot, the conveyance by lot and block number will convey the fee interest to the middle of the street.

Texas Bitulithic Company v. Warwick[10] demonstrates this principle. The City of Waxahachie sued the Warwicks for collection of a special assessment for paving the street in front of their home. The paving company intervened, seeking enforcement of its mechanics lien. But the work the paving company had done was in the street and not on the house itself. The Warwicks claimed the lien was unenforceable against their homestead, pointing out that their deed described their property as abutting the street but did not purport to convey any part of the street. The Warwicks lost,

---

[9] *Rio Bravo Oil Co. v. Weed*, 50 S.W.2d 1080 (Tex. 1932); *Miller v. Cretien*, 488 S.W.2d 893 (Tex. Civ. App.—Fort Worth 1972, writ ref'd n.r.e.); *Gulf Sulphur Co. v. Ryman*, 221 S.W. 310 (Tex. Civ. App.—Galveston 1920, no writ).

[10] 293 S.W. 160 (Tex. Comm'n App. 1927, judgm't adopted).

because their deed conveyed to them fee title to the middle of the street even though the deed did not mention it.[11]

Texas Bitulithic Company v. Warwick was cited as recently as 1990 for the same principle in a case involving claims to oil and gas under a highway.[12] The court stated that the rule was well established that abutting owners own to the middle of the public right-of-way.

There may, however, be a contrary rule when the subdivider signing a plat is itself a city and not a private party.[13] In contrast, when the State of Texas grants lands bordering upon a street or highway, the general rule is that the grant "is to be construed in the same manner as grants between individuals."[14]

Humble Oil & Refining Co. v. Blankenburg[15] directly addressed the nature of the interest conveyed by a plat dedication. The Charlotte Townsite Company filed a plat in 1911 for the town of Charlotte, setting apart and dedicating "to the use of the public forever the plazas, parks, streets and alleys" shown on the plat.[16] Humble claimed the minerals under the plazas, parks, streets, and alleys based on a conveyance from a successor-in-interest to the Charlotte Townsite Company. But the town of Charlotte gave a mineral lease to a man named Atkins. The Texas Supreme Court

---

[11] *Id.* at 162.
[12] *Krenek v. Texastar N. Am., Inc.,* 787 S.W.2d 566 (Tex. App.—Corpus Christi 1990, writ denied).
[13] *Guenther v. Thompson,* 199 S.W.2d 710, 710 (Tex. Civ. App.—San Antonio 1947, no writ).
[14] *Joslin v. State,* 146 S.W.2d 208, 211 (Tex. Civ. App.—Austin 1940, writ ref'd).
[15] 235 S.W.2d 891 (Tex. 1951).
[16] *Id.* at 893.

affirmed that the Charlotte Townsite plat conveyed only an easement to the town. The company had retained the fee, including all minerals. Thus, Humble's claim prevailed over Atkins'.

Platted streets are typically easement streets.

2.02.02. Exceptions to the General Rule.

It may be possible for a plat to expressly convey to the city the fee under streets or other rights-of-way. That said, it is unlikely and undesirable. No city should permit it, but it is difficult to say such a conveyance is impossible.

A more likely exception to the ownership-to-the-middle rule concerns platted streets or other easements immediately abutting the edge of a platted subdivision. Imputation of fee ownership under a street or other easement works only within a plat. Another exception is when the easement or easements are large in relation to the size of the abutting property.

In the first case, imagine a street or, more likely, a drainage easement running along the edge of a platted subdivision. When the plat is first filed, the entire platted area typically belongs to the subdivider. There's no ordinary expectation that owners of property outside the plat own property inside the plat. For part of the perimeter easement to belong to people outside the plat, the plat itself would have to operate as a conveyance to the outside owners. That would be nonsensical. Instead, subject to the next exception, the fee ownership of the abutting owners inside the subdivision extends all the way to the plat boundary. Instead of owning the fee to the middle of the easement, the owners who abut inside the subdivision own the fee all the way across to the subdivision boundary. The owners who abut outside the subdivision get nothing.

This principle was referred to in *Cantley v. Gulf Production Co.*,[17] a case involving a dedication of a road allegedly never opened.

Another exception is when the value of the fee under the easement is more than should pass by implication. The Texas Supreme Court considered such a scenario in *Haines v. McLean*.[18] The facts are convoluted and are simplified here to get to the principle.

William McLean owned the entire tract shown in the nearby figure. The tract was transected by three diagonal easements, the three easternmost strips in the figure. In 1924, McLean conveyed all the land to Grabow. In 1929, Grabow conveyed the eastern tract to Yoder. When Grabow did so, he described the western boundary of the conveyance as the eastern boundary of the easements. Yoder later conveyed to the Boothes with the same description. After that, the property west of the easements passed to the Haines. Then the parties disputed who owned the fee under the three easements.

Consistently with principles discussed in this handbook, the Texas Supreme Court held that the Boothes owned the fee under the eastern half of the three eastern easements. Describing the western boundary of the conveyance as the eastern boundary

---

17   143 S.W.2d 912 (Tex. 1940).
18   276 S.W.2d 777 (Tex. 1955).

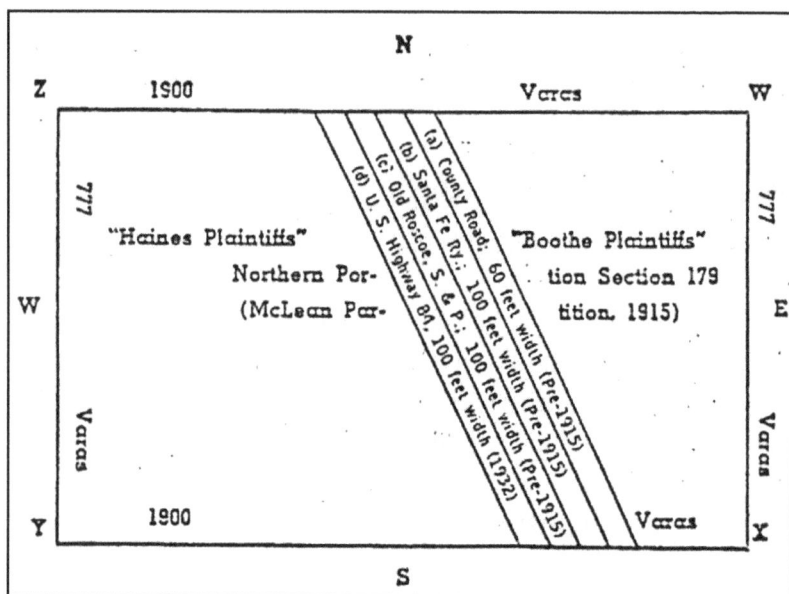

of the easements merely reserved the easements. It did not retain the fee under the easements for Grabow or Yoder.

The difficulty came on the west side. In 1932, Grabow heirs conveyed the fourth and westernmost strip in fee to Scurry County for road purposes. The question was whether Scurry County had succeeded to ownership of the fee under the western half of the three easements. But the western half of the three easements was a larger area than the road tract conveyed to Scurry County. Scurry County getting ownership of a larger tract merely because of its acquisition of the road strip shocked the court's conscience. Accordingly, the Haines retained ownership of the fee under the three easement strips.[19] Thus, the size of fee ownership under

---

[19] *Id.* at 786.

easements cannot be excessive in relation to the size of the abutting fee-owned tract for the fee under the easement to be imputed to the abutting tract.

Similar facts arose in *Angelo v. Biscamp*.[20] In 1956, Mr. and Mrs. Angelo acquired five lots in a Beaumont subdivision. Each of the lots was 25 feet by 140 feet. The lot on one end abutted a 50-foot-wide railroad easement. While the Angelos owned the lots, the railroad right-of-way was abandoned, and then the Angelos sold the lots without reference to the railroad right-of-way. The question was whether the fee under the former railroad right-of-way passed to the buyers or was retained by the Angelos.

The court noted that the former railroad right-of-way was commercially valuable. Further, the relevant segment was 50 feet by 140 feet, twice the size of the lot it abutted. The court rendered judgment that the Angelos retained ownership of the former right-of-way.

The result in *Angelo v. Biscamp* is consistent with general principles concerning the strip-and-gore doctrine, but the case does not discuss how the Angelos got title to the right-of-way. It would seem anomalous for them to have gotten it by strip-and-gore doctrine when they purchased the subject lots. Perhaps the explanation is as simple as that no other claimants were before the court. The buyers, who were claiming through the Angelos, were not going to assert that the Angelos never got title.

---

[20] 441 S.W.2d 524 (Tex. 1969)

West Publishing's one-paragraph synopsis at the beginning of the case implies that the timing of railroad abandonment is significant. The railroad abandoned the right-of-way after the Angelos acquired title and before they sold to others, but that implication is not in the opinion of the court. And the strip-and-gore doctrine does not typically depend on whether the strip or gore is burdened with an easement.

2.03. Ancient Roads.

Before there were roads as we know them, there were tracks through the wilderness. These tracks may have begun as game trails or simply as convenient paths between two settlements. As an area settled, these ways became more established roads.

Ancient roads, as they are known, are likely more common in rural areas. Development in cities may alter the routes of all but the most established roads. Whether urban or rural, ancient roads are typically considered to exist by easement.[21]

2.04. San Antonio's Historical Streets.

San Antonio's history creates a potential exception to the easement rule. In 1731, in the name of the King of Spain, the Spanish Viceroy made a large land grant to the village of San Fernando de Béxar,[22] the predecessor-in-interest to present-day San Antonio. The interest granted by the Viceroy is treated today as that of a fee.

---

[21] *O'Connor v. Gragg*, 339 S.W.2d 878 (Tex. 1960).
[22] The Spanish pronunciation of "Béxar" is BAY har, which is how "Bexar" came to be pronounced as "bear."

According to lore, when San Fernando sold off most of its grant to private owners, it reserved strips for streets in between the parcels sold. Since San Fernando had owned the entire grant in fee, if San Fernando retained the strips, it retained the fee in the strips. But taking the lore at face value, we cannot assume all old streets consist of the retained strips. The lore also holds that the tracts originally sold were large enough that intervening streets had to be laid out. The intervening streets would likely exist by easement. Thus, only some old streets would have been fee streets.

It's hard to know which streets are which, given that the earliest generally available map showing any significant level of street detail is dated 1852. That is more than 100 years after the founding of San Fernando de Béxar. Few records for the period before 1836 are available, most likely because of disruption arising from the Texas revolution. Several witnesses in the early case of *City of San Antonio v. Samuel Kinny* testified that pre-1836 records were destroyed in the Texas revolution, though whether by the forces of Santa Anna or of General Cos or of the Americans is unclear.[23]

It's also hard to reconstruct how such streets might have been rerouted in the intervening almost 300 years. If rerouted, the documents associated with the rerouting would control the ownership of the streets. Correspondingly, if widened, the documents associated with the widening would control the ownership of the widening strips. According to historical documents, the original streets were 13⅓ varas wide.[24] Given that a vara is 33⅓ inches

---

[23] Suit-related materials are recorded at Volume 1011, Page 385-412, Deed Records of Bexar County, Texas.

[24] Lota M. Spell, *The Grant and First Survey of the City of San Antonio*, 66 Sw. Hist. Q. 73, 84 (1963).

long,[25] the original streets were approximately 37 feet wide. That is quite narrow for a modern street, so the original streets have almost certainly been widened if not rerouted.

Early events in San Antonio were discussed in *Lewis v. City of San Antonio*.[26] Similarly, the early history of Refugio is discussed in *Town of Refugio v. Byrne*[27] and *Heard v. Town of Refugio*.[28] The founding of Laredo is discussed in *City of Laredo v. De Moreno*.[29]

Given that San Antonio has these difficulties, take pity on the municipal real estate lawyers in older cities. Whatever William of Normandy may have preserved in London, it seems unlikely that street record preservation was a priority for the Huns in Rome or the Saracens in Constantinople.

2.05. Widened or Rerouted Streets.

When a street is widened or rerouted, the city must acquire rights in the new area. The area can be acquired by easement or in fee.

If it is acquired in easement, the principles relating to platted streets still pertain, except that line at which abutting owners' fee ownership meets will be the original middle of the street. If, in widening the street, the city takes equal amounts from both sides,

---

[25] Tex. Nat. Res. Code Ann. § 21.077(3) (West 2011).
[26] 7 Tex. 288 (1851).
[27] 25 Tex. 193 (1860).
[28] 103 S.W.2d 728 (Tex. 1938).
[29] 183 S.W. 827 (Tex. Civ. App.—San Antonio 1916, no writ).

then the original middle of the street and the middle as widened will be identical. But if the widening requires taking more from one side of the street than the other, the original middle and the middle as widened differ. Abutting owners do not gain or lose any fee interest because one of them conveyed more easement to the city. The owners will own to the original middle.[30]

Acquiring a widening strip in fee when the underlying street exists by easement creates a confusing pattern of ownership and a legal issue that might have to be resolved in litigation. Though the pre-existing fee ownership is neatly divided at the centerline of the old street, a fee acquisition sets up intervening ownership of a small strip. See the later discussion at Section 7.03 (Avoiding Patchwork of Ownership).

A rerouted street segment purchased in fee does not present the title-confusion issue that a widening strip does, but it is still undesirable. See the discussion at Section 7 (Should Public Street Right-of-Way be Acquired in Fee or by Easement?).

2.06. Interest of Property Owners in Streets.

When lots are sold under a subdivision plat, the purchasers acquire an ingress-egress easement in the streets shown on the plat whether or not the streets ever actually are built and the city accepts them. *Dykes v. City of Houston*[31] offers a good example.

---

[30] *cf, Haines v. McLean*, 276 S.W.2d 777 (Tex. 1955).
[31] 406 S.W.2d 176 (Tex. 1966).

Mr. Dykes bought a lot in the Bayou Woods Subdivision, which was later annexed by the City of Houston. The subdivision streets never were improved and were overgrown. When Houston would not improve the streets, Mr. Dykes removed vegetation and graded the street to his lot. Houston then erected a wooden barricade to prevent access. Mr. Dykes burned the barricade, so Houston erected a metal one. Mr. Dykes was taking down the metal barricade with a blowtorch when the police came.

Houston argued that the barricade was necessary for public safety. Without it, someone not familiar with the area might drive off the end of the pavement into the dirt. The court recognized that cities have the right to control streets generally and to determine whether to improve them. Houston was not required to improve Bayou Woods streets. But Mr. Dykes and other lot owners had easement rights to get to their lots.

The Texas Supreme Court noted a Houston ordinance allowing petitions to city council for leave for laying out and clearing streets, and ruled that Mr. Dykes should follow that procedure. The court went on to state that, if the city said no, Mr. Dykes would be entitled to further relief. Perhaps Houston got the message, because the case does not appear further in the reporter.

Bowers v. Machir[32] is another case touching on the same issue. The city council of the City of Fort Worth passed an alley-closure ordinance stating that the alley "is hereby ordered closed and the right to the use of the said alley is hereby granted and vested" in

---

[32] 191 S.W. 758 (Tex. Civ. App.—San Antonio 1916, no writ).

the abutting owners. The abutting owners built a fence, and other nearby owners sued for its removal.

Despite the language of the ordinance, the court stated that the alley was closed only by the fence erected by the abutting owners. The effect of the ordinance was not a closure but only a relinquishment of public rights in the alley. Specifically, despite the closure ordinance, the city had no right to prevent use of the alley by those having a private right to do so.[33] The judgment in favor of Fort Worth was reversed and remanded.

Owners of lots in the subdivision creating a street may have private rights in the street whether or not the city enforces public rights.

———

[33] *Id.* at 761.

3. What Is the Difference Between Streets and Alleys?

Alleys are narrow streets. Cities often set different minimum widths for alleys as compared to streets. The City of San Antonio is one such city.[34] The minimum width is the only difference.

Kalteyer v. Sullivan[35] addressed precisely this point. With the City of San Antonio's permission, Sullivan installed gates at both ends of an alley running behind Kalteyer's property. Kalteyer sued to remove the gates. Sullivan replied that the city had given permission for the gates and that Kalteyer had another way to come and go.

The court stated that any way over land set apart for public travel in a town or city is a street. The way may be called a street, an alley,

---

[34] San Antonio, Tex., Unified Development Code § 35-506 tbl.506-3 (2006).

[35] 18 Tex. Civ. App. 488, 46 S.W. 288 (San Antonio 1898, writ ref'd).

or a highway, but the rules are the same. The court also noted that "a narrow way, less in size than a street, is generally called an alley."[36] The court required the gates to come down.

Greer v. Robertson[37] is another case addressing the equivalence between streets and alleys. One neighbor erected a fence blocking the alley, and another neighbor objected. The court found the alley to be a public street, so that erection of a fence blocking the alley was wrongful.

———

---

[36] *Id.* at 493, 46 S.W. at 290.
[37] 297 S.W.2d 279 (Tex. Civ. App.—Fort Worth 1956, writ ref'd n.r.e.).

4. What Is the Difference Between Urban Streets and Rural Roads?

None. Just as the rights pertaining to alleys are identical to those pertaining to streets, the rights pertaining to rural roads are identical to those pertaining to city streets.[38]

Consider the problems if the rule were otherwise. Streets and roads are defined by property interests divided between the state (the holder of the street right-of-way easement) and the abutting owners (the holders of the fee underlying the street right-of-way easement). If the division for rural roads were different from that for city streets, a city's acts of annexation and deannexation would affect vested property rights. Eventually, courts would be dealing with claims that an annexation or deannexation was a regulatory taking.

------

[38] *Hill Farm, Inc. v. Hill Cnty.*, 436 S.W.2d 320, 323 (Tex. 1969); *Blackburn v. Brazos Valley Utils., Inc.*, 777 S.W.2d 758, 761 (Tex. App.—Beaumont 1989, writ denied).

5. Should Utility Easements Run Alongside Streets?

5.01. Background.

No. Public utilities have the right to put their lines and other infrastructure in the public street right-of-way, though they may not block the public's travel. This authority is statutory. There is a specific authorization for each type of utility: water and sewer,[39] gas,[40] electric,[41] and telephone and telegraph[42] utilities. Cable television companies can use the streets in unincorporated areas[43] and in incorporated ones if they obtain a franchise from the Public Utilities Commission.[44]

---

[39] Tex. Loc. Gov't Code Ann. §§ 552.103–.104 (West Supp. 2013); Tex. Water Code Ann. § 49.220 (West 2008).

[40] Tex. Util. Code Ann. §§ 181.005 (West Supp. 2013), 181.006 (West 2007).

[41] *Id.* §§ 181.042–.043 (West 2007).

[42] *Id.* § 181.082.

[43] *Id.* § 181.102.

[44] *Id.* § 66.003.

Public utilities, however, often resist putting their lines in public streets. Instead, they attempt to influence the platting process, requiring separate utility easements to run alongside public streets. Why is that? Money.

Someone has to pay when the city's street work requires utility lines to be relocated or otherwise disturbed. If the utilities are in the street, the general rule is that utilities pay. But if the utilities have their own easement, then the city's encroachment on the easement is an infringement on the utilities' property rights. So the city pays.

The rule for utilities in streets is illustrated in *City of San Antonio v. Bexar Metropolitan Water District.*[45] The water district laid water lines in county roads. When the city annexed the area, it improved the county roads, which became city streets by virtue of the annexation. The street improvement required the water district's lines to be moved, and the water district resisted paying the cost. The city sued and prevailed.

A similar principle worked in favor of the City of San Antonio's water utility in an earlier case, *City of San Antonio v. San Antonio Street-Railway Co.*[46] The street-railway company sought to stop construction of sewer lines down streets where the street-railway company already had tracks. The court found that streets are fundamentally public. Other uses such as street railways are subordinate to the public right, and the street-railway company had a

---

[45] 309 S.W.2d 491 (Tex. Civ. App—San Antonio 1958, writ ref'd).
[46] 15 Tex. Civ. App. 1, 39 S.W. 136 (San Antonio 1896, writ ref'd).

right to use the street only until the public needed the street.[47] The court therefore denied the street-railway company compensation for the removal of its tracks.

As each type of utility has a separate statute entitling it to use of the streets, there are separate statutes or other bases of authority to require utilities to bear the cost of relocating lines necessitated by street improvements: telecommunications,[48] cable television in rural areas,[49] cable television in municipalities,[50] electric lines inside a city,[51] electric lines outside a city,[52] gas,[53] water and wastewater inside a city,[54] and water and wastewater outside a city.[55]

Utilities try to maneuver cities into paying for relocation. Cities should reciprocate, cities and utilities each trying to get in the other's pocket. Property owners trying to get a plat filed are pawns in this fight, but they have a stake, too. If utilities succeed in getting an easement running alongside the street, more of the owner's property is undevelopable, which reduces the value of the property. So utilities are imposing an expense on owners to avoid an expense themselves. That additional expense is an exaction.

---

[47] *Id.* at 8, 39 S.W. at 139.
[48] Tex. Util. Code Ann. § 54.203 (West 2007).
[49] *Id.* § 181.104.
[50] 47 U.S.C. § 541(a)(2) (2006).
[51] Common law rule.
[52] Tex. Util. Code Ann. § 181.046 (West 2007).
[53] *Id.* § 104.112.
[54] Tex. Water Code Ann. § 13.247 (West Supp. 2013).
[55] Tex. Loc. Gov't Code Ann. § 552.105 (West Supp. 2013).

5.02. Exactions.

Exactions are conditions government places on development and are generally beyond the scope of this handbook. But in short, if a city places conditions on development, there must be an essential nexus between those conditions and a legitimate state interest. Further, the required infrastructure dedications must be roughly proportionate to the infrastructure burden created by the proposed development. If an exaction fails one of these tests, it is a constitutionally compensable taking.

A landmark exaction case arose in Ventura County, California, where a family named Nollan owned beachfront property. In 1982, the Nollans applied for a permit to replace a small bungalow with a three-bedroom house. The California Coastal Commission conditioned the permit on the Nollans granting a public easement along the beach. The Commission justified this condition on the house blocking the view of the beach from the public street. In *Nollan v. California Coastal Commission*,[56] the U.S. Supreme Court found the condition to be an uncompensated taking. That was because the restriction, dedication of a beach easement, bore no essential nexus to the burden caused by the development, a blocked view.

The potential for taking-related liability was expanded when the owner of an electrical supply store in Tigard, Oregon, applied for a permit to expand and to pave the parking lot. The City of Tigard granted the permit on the condition that the owner dedicate a greenway along a nearby creek and build a hike and bike path to relieve congestion. These conditions were upheld throughout the

---

[56] 428 U.S. 825 (1987).

Oregon court system, and the owner appealed to the U.S. Supreme Court. In *Dolan v. City of Tigard*,[57] the Supreme Court found an essential nexus, but the City of Tigard lost because the conditions were not roughly proportionate to the increased burden imposed by the proposed improvements to the electrical supply store. Thus, to avoid liability for a taking, both (A) an essential nexus must exist between the condition imposed and the harm to be remedied, and (B) the conditions imposed must be roughly proportionate to the burden created by the development.

5.03. Essential Nexus Between Development and Utility Installations.

In areas being newly developed, an essential nexus will often exist between new development and the need for new places to install utilities. But when a parcel in a developed area is being redeveloped, utility lines are usually already in the street. In such a case, it is harder to see a nexus between replatting a parcel and having to dedicate more of the property for utilities.

5.04. Rough Proportionality of Requirement for Separate Easement.

Both with new development and with redevelopment of previously developed areas, utilities have a pre-existing right to be in the street. So the need for utilities is met. Would requiring an additional utility easement alongside a street be proportionate to

---

[57] 512 U.S. 374 (1994).

the burden a development places on public infrastructure? It is always easier to answer such questions in the context of specific facts, but most of the time the streets will be adequate to provide necessary utility service. When the dedication of the street is adequate for installing utilities, requiring a further dedication seems disproportionate to the burden imposed by the property owner's plans.

Utilities don't demand space additional to the street for utilities because they need it to provide utility service. They demand it to avoid future expense. That is, they impose an immediate cost on property owners to avoid a hypothetical future cost for themselves.

5.05. Potential Liability for a Regulatory Taking.

Cities that accommodate utilities' desires for separate easements running alongside streets not only cost themselves money when future roadwork is necessary; they are also potentially subjecting themselves to liability to developers for unconstitutional takings. Why would anyone at a city agree to that? Perhaps partly because those involved do not grasp the larger picture, and partly because acceding to the utilities is the path of least resistance. The problem created will most often arise only later and for someone else at the city, not the officials in charge of the plat approval process. Of course, if a property owner makes a takings claim, the path of least resistance may change.

6. Does the Term "Right-of-Way" Mean the City Owns the Fee?

No. In fact, when the term "right-of-way" appears on a plat with no other explanation, it creates an easement. This remains true despite the persistence of the urban legend in the San Antonio real estate community to the contrary.

Stanbury v. Wallace[58] stated that "if the granting clause of a deed conveys a right-of-way over land for street purposes, it will not be held to convey the fee." Other cases have looked to the language of the specific deed to tell whether the parties intended a fee or an easement conveyance.[59] In the cases finding a fee conveyance, the finding was based on language in the deed apart from the deed's use of the term "right-of-way." Plats typically do not and should not contain language that would cause such a deviation.

---

[58] 45 S.W.2d 198 (Tex. Comm'n App. 1932, judgm't adopted).
[59] *Lakeside Launches, Inc. v. Austin Yacht Club, Inc.*, 750 S.W.2d 868 (Tex. App.—Austin 1988, writ denied); *Hidalgo Cnty v. Pate*, 443 S.W.2d 80 (Tex. Civ. App.—Corpus Christi 1969, writ ref'd n.r.e.).

For example, compare *Right of Way Oil Co. v. Gladys City, Oil, Gas & Mfg. Co.*[60] with *Texas Electric Ry. Co. v. Neale.*[61] Right of Way Oil Co. claimed the right to minerals under the railroad right-of-way based on rights obtained from the railroad. Gladys City, which had a deed to the property, claimed the railroad did not get the right to the oil and gas under its right-of-way. To determine the scope of rights obtained by the railroad, the court looked at the conveyance clause of the railroad deed. That clause did not purport to convey the land but only a right-of-way over it.[62] The court concluded that conveying a right-of-way amounted to conveyance of only an easement. The railroad easement did not include a right to the minerals.

In contrast, Texas Electric Ry. Co. claimed through a deed in which the grantors stated that "by these presents [we do] grant, sell and convey unto [the grantees] their successors and assigns, the following described piece or parcel of land . . ."[63] Though the same deed later required the grantees to build a railway, the court found that the deed purported to convey the land itself and not a right-of-way over it. The requirement to build a railroad did not change the intent to convey the fee.

Interestingly, the court in *Texas Electric Ry. Co.* cited and distinguished *Right of Way Oil Co. v. Gladys City, Oil, Gas & Mfg. Co.* by noting that, in the latter case, the deed explicitly stated that it conveyed a right-of-way.[64] Thus in these two cases, the Texas

---

[60] 157 S.W. 737 (Tex. 1913).

[61] 252 S.W.2d 451 (Tex. 1952).

[62] 157 S.W. at 739.

[63] 252 S.W.2d at 452.

[64] *Id.* at 455.

Supreme Court has made clear that a deed conveying a right-of-way conveys an easement, while one conveying the land conveys the fee. There is no rational basis to conclude that the term "right-of-way" on a plat denotes a fee interest.

The Texas Supreme Court more recently touched on right-of-way in *State of Texas v. NICO-WF1, LLC*.[65] The issue was not whether the street was an easement. Instead, it was whether the width of Arroyo Boulevard in Los Fresnos, Texas, extended the full width of the area between the right-of-way lines, as the state contended. The abutting owner, whose improvements extended beyond the right-of-way line but stopped short of the curb, argued the state's rights are limited to the narrower width between the curbs. In holding for the state, the court used the terms "right-of-way" and "easement" interchangeably.

Despite the above, the belief that right-of-way means fee is entrenched and long lasting. In discussing this issue in a paper prepared in the 1990s, former San Antonio Deputy City Attorney Jackson Hubbard noted that the confusion has persisted for 100 years and is not abating. He cautioned surveyors to carefully assess the character of any right-of-way interest they encounter in their work and cautioned lawyers to be careful to make their intentions clear in drafting documents. The cautions remain appropriate.

———

[65] 384 S.W.3d 818 (Tex. 2012).

7. Should Right-of-Way Be Acquired in Fee or by Easement?

7.01. Arguments in Favor of Acquiring an Easement.

A properly drafted public street right-of-way easement gives a city all the rights it needs for a public street. Taking the street in fee burdens a city with problems it would not have with an easement. An aggressive owner might defeat an attempted condemnation of the fee for street widening, because the fee is more than the city is likely to need.

7.01.01. Maintenance of Unpaved Portions of the Right-of-Way.

Not all the public right-of-way is paved. Part of it is often grass or other landscaping. Cities often require abutting landowners to maintain the landscaping.[66] Cities also often require abutting

---

[66] *See, e.g.,* San Antonio, Tex., Code of Ordinances § 29-11 (1986).

owners to maintain sidewalks.[67] The rationale is that the abutting owner owns the fee under the easement. If the city and not the abutter owns the fee, the rationale for imposing these duties on an abutter becomes thin.

7.01.02. Liability of City for Unsafe Conditions.

Clearly, the city is liable for unsafe conditions relating to street uses of the right-of-way. But again, not all the right-of-way is paved, and adjoining owners may create unsafe conditions for pedestrians in the unpaved portions. For example, if an abutting owner digs a hole and allows it to become obscured with tall weeds, a pedestrian could be injured falling into the hole. If all the city has is an easement and the hole is not related to street activity, the city will not likely be liable. If the city owns the fee, the city's defenses are fewer. These conditions can be difficult to police.

It's true that the city will be able to assert governmental immunity to many suits and will find its liability limited by the Tort Claims Act in others, but not being liable in the first place is the best defense.

7.01.03. Avoiding Patchwork of Ownership.

Because streets exist mostly by easement, acquiring expanded right-of-way in fee creates a confusing patchwork of unusable fee ownerships scattered around the city. No development or right-of-way is forever, and city fee ownership would complicate redevelopment of the area. No one should want that. Imagine trying to sort out who owns what 250 years from now.

---

[67] *See, e.g., id.* § 29-193.

In evaluating this point, consider Figure 1.

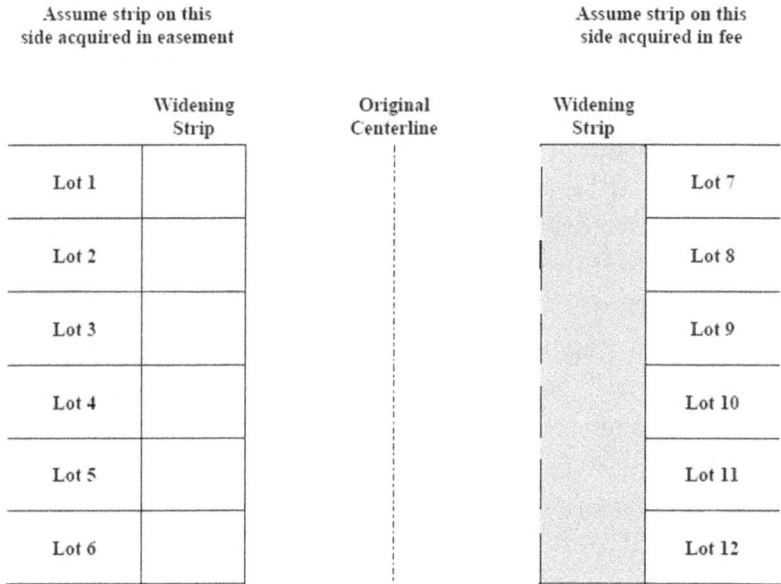

Figure 1

Figure 1 shows a street on which a city has acquired widening strips on both sides. The strip on the left was acquired by easement, and the one on the right was acquired in fee. On the left side, the owner of Lot 1 still owns the fee under the street easement all the way to the original centerline. The same principle applies down the line of lots on the left.

On the right side, the city owns the fee to the shaded strip. Ownership of the fee between the shaded strip and the original centerline is unclear. The owner of Lot 7 may continue to own the fee between the shaded strip and the original centerline. On the other hand, a court might hold that the fee between the shaded strip and the centerline has become an appurtenance of the ownership of the shaded strip. The same principle applies down the line of lots to the right.

The widening strip (the shaded tract) will often be small in relation to the width of the old street bed (possibly alleged to be appurtenant to the shaded tract). The apparent width in Figure 1 is exaggerated. Under the strip-and-gore doctrine, the strip or gore that passes to the new owner should be small in relation to the tract to which the strip or gore is alleged to be appurtenant. In a typical street widening, the widening strip will be significantly smaller than half the width of the original street. That's the reverse of the facts often relied on to invoke the strip-and-gore doctrine. See *Haines v. McLean*,[68] which is discussed in Section 2.02.02 (Exceptions to the General Rule).

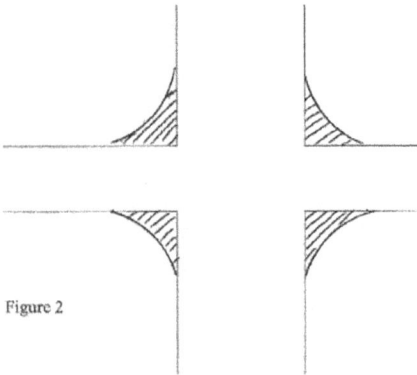

Figure 2

Intersection improvements present even worse facts than street widenings. All the city often takes is a point at each corner to allow for turn lanes. These tracts present an odd pattern of fee ownership. See Figure 2.

Cities have to take the long view. Eventually, even if it is many decades, all areas will be redeveloped. Then, if not before, someone

---

[68] 276 S.W.2d 777 (Tex. 1955).

will need to settle who owns what in areas where streets have been improved. When a city has acquired interests in fee, it may be necessary to resolve ownership in court. No lawyer should want to create a situation where that is necessary.

7.01.04. *Environmental Liability.*

The owner of a fee interest is potentially liable for all environmental contamination on his property whether or not the owner caused it. An easement holder may be able to escape liability for contamination if it appears that the contamination is unrelated to the holder's use of the easement. This is a significant reason never to take the fee to any real property you don't need to own. A city buying street right-of-way in fee unnecessarily exposes itself and the taxpayers to liability for contamination by past owners.

7.01.05. *Illegal Subdivision.*

When buying a widening strip in fee, we sever the strip from the tract to which it formerly belonged. That is a subdivision. Except for subdivisions of five acres or more meeting criteria not generally relevant to streets, subdivisions should be replatted.[69] If the city has chosen to be regulated by Subchapter B of Chapter 212 of the Local Government Code, as San Antonio has done,[70] failure to replat when required to do so is a Class C misdemeanor. Each day the violation continues is a separate offense.[71] Widening strips will seldom be five acres or more.

---

[69] Tex. Loc. Gov't Code Ann. § 212.004 (West 2008).
[70] San Antonio, Tex., Unified Development Code § 35-433(a)(1) (2006).
[71] Tex. Loc. Gov't Code Ann. § 212.050(d) (West 2008).

Some cities may have an argument that widening strips acquired in fee need not be platted. Cities may create exceptions to platting requirements.[72] By so doing, cities have the ability to exempt themselves from some platting rules.

One may argue that the City of San Antonio has exempted itself from the need to replat when acquiring widening strips, because its Unified Development Code platting requirements exempt some tracts acquired for public infrastructure.[73] Public streets are public infrastructure. But the relevant provision of the Unified Development Code[74] is limited to unplatted parcels. Most widening strips are acquired from platted parcels. Thus, San Antonio's exception does not apply to most acquisitions.

Whether or not replatting is required at the time a widening strip is severed from its parent tract, the seller or his successor is likely to have to replat his property some day. Possible reasons are a sale to a buyer who requires it or a loan from a bank that requires it. This hidden need to replat will result in significant expense. Cities may be reluctant to disclose the prospective expense to owners, because doing so would discourage owner cooperation. Taking advantage of citizens' ignorance is unfair.

When a city insists on buying a widening strip in fee, the seller should insist that the city replat the seller's property as part of the transaction. In addition to avoiding future replatting expenses, replatting will also protect the owner from the problems discussed

---

[72] *Id.* § 212.0045(a).).

[73] San Antonio, Tex., Unified Development Code § 35-430(c)(5) (2006).

[74] *Id.* § 35-430.

at Section 7.06 (Street Access Rights of Abutting Owner). That assumes the entire parcel purchased by the city is dedicated on the replat as public street right-of-way.

It would be cheaper and more practical for the city to acquire only an easement. Then the owner does not suffer the hidden detriment of needing to replat.

7.01.06. Street Access Rights of Abutting Owners.

If the city acquires widening strips by street easement, abutting owners automatically have the right to access the public street subject to generally applicable curb-cut rules. In contrast, an owner selling the city a strip in fee along the property's street frontage has to trust the city to turn the entire strip into public street right-of-way. If the city uses only some of the strip for a public street right-of-way, the property owner may be cut off from access to the street.

Sometimes a lawyer representing a property owner will raise this issue, insisting on an ingress-egress easement across the strip being sold in fee. All lawyers representing property owners should do so, because the city's plans can change with the prevailing political winds. But a reserved ingress-egress easement is a problem for the city. That's because the property owner may later argue that the reserved easement is an exemption from curb-cut rules, entitling the owner to driveways in otherwise prohibited locations. Curb cuts may create public safety hazards depending on their number and where they are, so it's undesirable for owners to be exempt from curb-cut rules. The problem is easily finessed by the city acquiring the strip by easement instead of in fee.

As noted above at Section 7.05 (Illegal Subdivision), an owner's street access may also be preserved by requiring the city to replat the property the widening strip is acquired from, but only if the entire parcel purchased is dedicated as public street right-of-way. Assuring that detail in the final plat may be difficult, so the careful practitioner may nevertheless want to insist on an ingress-egress easement across the strip sold.

A similar problem arose in a different and more extreme context for owners of land around Medina Lake, which is located northwest of San Antonio. The lake was created in the early 1900s with a maximum elevation of 1,084 feet. Of course, given erratic rainfall in Central Texas, the lake is seldom that high. As of this writing, the lake is nearly dry. The lake owner claimed fee ownership to the 1,084 contour line. The homeowners claimed the right to water access. The dispute was ultimately settled, but if the lakebed had been acquired by inundation easement instead of in fee, the dispute would have been at least partly avoided, depending the location of pre-existing property lines below the 1,084 contour line. While not street related, the Medina Lake access disputes show by analogy what could happen to a property owner selling a fee strip between his property and the public street.

State v. Fuller[75] presents the problem in a street-related context. A railroad right-of-way ran between Fuller's land and U.S. 69, which was owned in fee by the State of Texas. As abutting fee owners, Fuller and the state each owned half the fee under the railroad right-of-way.

---

[75] 407 S.W.2d 215 (Tex. 1966).

When the railroad ceased operating and abandoned its easement, Fuller wanted to cross over the former railroad easement to get access to U.S. 69. But the state owned half the former easement between Fuller and the highway. The state planned to expand U.S. 69 to encompass its half of the former railroad easement, but it had not yet done so at the time of the litigation. Because of the intervening state ownership, Fuller did not abut the highway and therefore did not to have a right to access it.[76]

It is unlikely that this problem would arise in any given fee acquisition of a widening strip, but why would a property owner want to assume the risk, however small, when the problem is so easily avoided by selling only an easement or requiring the city to plat the entire strip as public street?

7.01.07. Restrictive Covenants and POA Assessments.

Buying lots or strips from lots in subdivisions with property-owner associations presents additional problems. Sometimes subdivision covenants except property owned by governmental authorities. Sometimes not.

When property owned by governmental authorities is not excepted, when a city buys the fee, it may find itself burdened by these restrictions and, perhaps even worse, may have to pay assessments. If a city needs the fee, it can avoid this result by joining both the owner and the property-owner association in a condemnation. But condemnations entail delay and expense and are not favored

---

[76] *Id.* at 221.

politically. As a result, cities are often reluctant to condemn when they have an agreement on price with the owner.

Subdivision restrictions and assessments are typically imposed on owners of lots. If a city buys only an easement, someone else owns the fee and is therefore the lot owner. Thus, the city will often avoid restrictions and assessments.

7.02. Arguments in Favor of Acquiring in Fee.

7.02.01. Will Owners Have to Pay More Property Taxes If Left With the Fee?

An often-heard argument is that, if a city buys only an easement, the abutting owner's property taxes will be higher. Not so.

Texas ad valorem taxation must be equal and uniform,[77] so standards should be consistent across the state. Owners pay tax only on market value.[78] For ad valorem tax purposes, market value is defined as the price at which a property would transfer for cash or its equivalent under prevailing market conditions if:

a. Exposed for sale in the open market with a reasonable time for the seller to find a purchaser;

b. Both the seller and the purchaser know of all the uses and purposes the property is adapted to and which it is capable

---

[77] Tex. Const. art. 8, § 1.

[78] Tex. Tax Code Ann. § 23.01(a) (West Supp. 2013).

of being used for and of the enforceable restrictions on its use; and

c. Both the seller and purchaser seek to maximize their gains, and neither is in a position to take advantage of the exigencies of the other.[79]

There's no reason to suppose that market value is materially affected by whether the property includes ownership of the fee under an abutting street. Most property owners don't know they own to the centerline, and few buyers are likely to wonder whether they are getting the fee under the street in addition to the usable property. If sellers and buyers don't care, the matter can't have much effect on value. And if it doesn't affect value, it can't properly have much effect on taxes. It's possible that some appraisal district will try to jack up taxes on this basis, but there is no legal rationale for doing so. Tax appraisals are required to conform to generally accepted appraisal methods and techniques.[80]

7.02.02. Will Acquiring Just an Easement Impair the Ability of Utilities to Lay Their Lines in the Street?

No. If we acquire in fee, utilities have no right to place their lines without an express or implied street dedication. With a street dedication, whether fee or easement, utilities have all the rights they need. See the discussion at Section 5 (Should Utility Easements Run Alongside Streets?).

---

[79] *Id.* § 1.04(7); *see also Village Place, Ltd., v. VP Shopping, LLC*, 404 S.W.3d 115, 133 (Tex. App.—Houston [1st Dist.] 2013, no pet.).
[80] Tex. Tax Code Ann. § 23.01(b) (West Supp. 2013).

7.02.03. Will Owners of the Fee Under Right-of-Way Be Liable for Traffic Accidents or Street Defects?

No. Most streets are already easements, and as inventive as plaintiff lawyers can be, this assertion does not come up much. Further, torts generally fall into two categories: negligent and intentional. A person can't be negligent for not abating something that person doesn't control, so it's hard to imagine how an abutting owner is liable for failing to change how the city manages the streets. Property owners do not control cities. In contrast, if an owner intentionally injures someone, the owner is liable no matter who owns the fee.

7.02.04. Flexible Rights for Future Work.

As noted at Section 8.03 (Can Cities Allow Non-Street Uses by Abutting Owners?), when a city buys a street easement, owners of the underlying fee retain some rights. Sometimes the city may wish to expand the street or do additional work in a way that requires taking more rights from the fee owner. That means the city has to pay the fee owner more money.

For example, a man named Dunn owed two tracts, a small one with a well and a larger one for cultivation. U.S. 87 and a railroad right-of-way, which abutted U.S. 87, ran between the two tracts. Dunn ran an irrigation pipe from the well tract to the other, passing underneath the highway and the railroad. The state built Interstate 27 along U.S. 87, and condemned the tract with the well feeding Dunn's irrigation system.

In *State v. Dunn*,[81] the state contested Dunn's right to damages for loss of the well, arguing that Dunn did not have a right to run the pipes under the existing highway. But Dunn owned the fee under part of the rights-of-way and had a water-pipeline easement for the rest. Accordingly, Dunn successfully recovered damages for loss of the well. Had the state owned the fee under the entire highway, Dunn would not have been able to recover.

Couple the possibility of paying the fee owner more for future expansion with the original cost of the street easement. A comprehensively drafted street easement (see Sample A) costs about as much as a fee acquisition would. Thus, the possibility exists over time of paying more than the full market value of the property in question.

This is a rational concern, but even though this happened in *State v. Dunn*, it is not a likely occurrence. In addition, how fair is it for the city to take more rights from the fee owner than the city needs now, on the off chance that the city might someday need them? If the city does so, the detriment to the fee owner is immediate and the detriments to the city discussed in Sections 7.01 through 7.06 are also immediate. The benefit to the city is remote and speculative.

7.03. TxDOT Policy.

Admittedly, the Texas Department of Transportation generally chooses to buy right-of-way in fee contrary to the advice in this handbook. I am not privy to the reasoning of TxDOT officials, but their

---

[81] 574 S.W.2d 821 (Tex. Civ.App.—Amarillo 1978, writ ref'd n.r.e.).

rationale probably relates to cases such as *State v. Dunn*,[82] discussed in the preceding section. Whatever TxDOT's reasons may be, some of the factors discussed above apply to TxDOT and some largely do not.

Most TxDOT right-of-way is acquired in rural areas. Compelling farmers or ranchers to maintain anything outside their fences is probably politically unsustainable. That is a significant difference from urban areas where owners are expected to mow and remove litter all the way to the curb. The chances of environmental contamination in rural areas, while not zero, are less than in urban areas. Likewise, rural tracts are typically larger than urban ones, so the problem of illegal subdivisions will arise less often, though it doubtless will arise. The abutting-owner access-right issue is probably the same in rural areas as in urban ones, but the problem of irregular fee-ownership patterns is probably less merely because redevelopment is less likely.

Whether or not the above comparison is correct, TxDOT buys in fee, whereas this handbook recommends buying in easement. The reader can consider the issues and make a choice.

7.04. Sample Form.

A sample form for a public street right-of-way easement is attached as **Sample A**. It may be useful if you need to acquire corner clips or widening strips.

---

[82] *Id.*

Grantors have balked at the term "deed" for creating an easement, but deed is simply the name for an instrument that conveys an interest in real property. Thus, a deed is the appropriate instrument to create an easement, but it is sometimes expedient to delete the word "deed" so the transaction can proceed.

Grantors may seek to edit the deed to reserve special rights. But the form is intended to create the same set of rights as exist with platted streets. Edits to the form favoring grantors mean that the resulting street segment will, in some way, differ from a standard street. From the city's perspective, it is undesirable for any part of a street to differ from the rest. Further, some day in the future, city representatives will almost certainly assume no difference and act accordingly. Permitting edits to the form is to set a trap for the unwary.

No one at the city will want to condemn when there is an agreement on price and the dispute is among lawyers over mere words. If the grantor will not sign a standard form, however, the city ought to condemn to preserve the integrity of its streets.

———

8. Are Cities Free to Do Anything They Want With Public Streets?

8.01. Streets Are Held in Trust for the Public.

Property owners and others inconvenienced by a street or alley will frequently ask cities to close right-of-way, to permit encroachments onto it, or to permit special uses of it. In evaluating these requests, the dominant principle is that cities administer the public right-of-way in trust for the public.[83] This principle plays a role both in street closures and in considering proposed encroachments.

Texas Department of Transportation v. City of Sunset Valley[84] is a recent Texas Supreme Court case reaffirming the public trust principle. TxDOT closed a street that Sunset Valley had bought in its own

---

[83] *Bowers v. City of Taylor*, 24 S.W.2d 816, 817 (Tex. Comm'n App. 1930); *Texas Co. v. Texarkana Mach. Shops*, 1 S.W.2d 928, 931 (Tex. Civ. App.—Texarkana 1928, no writ); *City of San Antonio v. Rische*, 38 S.W. 388, 390 (Tex. Civ. App.—San Antonio 1896, writ ref'd).

[84] 146 S.W.3d 637 (Tex. 2004).

name. Sunset Valley sued but was not entitled to compensation, because cities have no proprietary rights in streets or rights of exclusive possession. Instead, cities are trustees for the state and for the public.[85]

Even given the public trust, many closures are in the public interest. Most cities have platted streets or street segments that have never been used and are likely never to be. Many alleys have fallen into disuse. A closure relieving the public of maintenance obligations is often a net public benefit.

Many minor encroachments may increase the quality of life in a city. Examples of usually benign right-of-way encroachments are features of zero-lot-line buildings such as cornices, awnings, and balconies extending over the sidewalk. Where sidewalks are wide enough, planters and even sidewalk cafes may improve the ambience of a city and make it a more desirable place to live.

But less benign uses are likely to arise. Many proposed private uses of the public right-of-way, whether in the form of an encroachment or a closure, will interfere with public use. A private use materially interfering with public use violates the public trust.

8.02. What Are the Issues in Closing Streets?

8.02.01. The Closure Must Have a Public Purpose.

In 1926, the City of Texarkana closed a segment of a public street. Thereafter, the Texas Company, the owner of fee underlying the

---

[85] *Id.* at 644–45.

street, built one or more structures on the street. Texarkana Machine Shops then sued to have the structures removed so that it could continue to use the street. In *Texas Co. v. Texarkana Machine Shops*,[86] the court conceded the city's power to close streets and then considered whether the particular closure was lawful. In so doing, the court noted that the street was still used by the general public or abutters and that the closure's primary purpose was to let the fee owner have unencumbered use of the property.[87]

The court set aside the closure, finding that street closures may be conducted only for the benefit of the public. The court first characterized a closure for private benefit as an abuse of power and later as an exercise of despotic power.[88]

In *Bowers v. City of Taylor*,[89] the city gave exclusive control of a street segment for 15 years to a railroad. The court found that the grant to the railroad was improper, stating, "The city is the trustee for the public, and . . . the City must always remain in a position to exercise its legislative power when required."[90] The court found the ordinance void, because it bartered away the city's legislative power, the power to regulate the streets.

In *Kalteyer v. Sullivan*,[91] the San Antonio City Council authorized Mr. Sullivan to block an alley with gates and to store building

---

[86] 1 S.W.2d 928 (Tex. Civ. App—Texarkana 1928, no writ).
[87] *Id.* at 930.
[88] *Id.* at 931.
[89] 24 S.W.2d 816 (Tex. Comm'n App. 1930).
[90] *Id.* at 817.
[91] 18 Tex. Civ. App. 488, 46 S.W. 288 (San Antonio 1898, writ ref'd).

material in the alley. The court pointed out that, apart from width, alleys are the same as streets,[92] and set aside the City Council action favoring Sullivan. In so doing, the court opined that the public should not have "to expect their trustees to become aiders and abettors of an individual in excluding them from and depriving them of the use of their highways." Rather, the public should be able to look to the council for protection from such things.[93]

Elston v. City of Panhandle[94] is another street closure case setting aside a closure for private benefit. The City of Panhandle closed a segment of a public street to facilitate building a railroad depot, which was found to be for a private purpose. The court explicitly noted that streets are held in public trust and found the closure to be ultra vires and void.[95] In refusing writ, the Supreme Court issued an opinion finding that the city and the railroad were joint tortfeasors.[96] The legislature has since enacted a statute protecting cities from liability for injunction and damages from one not abutting the closed segment,[97] but it has not altered the ultra vires aspect of what the City of Panhandle did.

It took the City of Dublin a couple of tries to understand the limits on its powers. In *Stevens v. City of Dublin*,[98] Stevens sued to stop closure of a block of College Street. The Dublin Independent School District owned all the property on both sides of the block

---

[92] *Id.* at 493–94, 46 S.W. at 290.

[93] *Id.* at 494, 46 S.W. at 290.

[94] 46 S.W.2d 420 (Tex. Civ. App.—Amarillo), *writ ref'd*, 50 S.W.2d 1090 (Tex. 1932).

[95] *Id.* 422.

[96] 50 S.W.2d 1090, 1090–91 (Tex. 1932).

[97] Tex. Civ. Prac. & Rem. Code Ann § 65.015 (West 2008).

[98] 169 S.W. 188 (Tex. Civ. App.—Fort Worth 1914, no writ).

closed. Stevens, therefore, neither abutted the closed segment nor any part of the block in which the segment was closed. But he did own property fronting on College Street that was immediately across Vallient, a cross street at which the closure stopped. The appellate court nevertheless referred to Stevens as an abutting owner and, in finding that the closure was not supported by an adequate public purpose, stated:

> In the case as here found the danger is to the school children, and arises only by their own seeking, so to speak, while trespassing upon a street which has been dedicated to other uses for the benefit of the general public. . . . Nor does it appear that reasonable regulations on the part of the proper authorities cannot be adopted that will prevent the children from seeking places of danger, and at the same time preserve the rights of the public and of abutting owners to the use of the street.[99]

It seems unlikely that a court today would take the same attitude toward school children, but today's traffic is probably quite different from that of 100 years ago. Further, a central element of the opinion was that Texas law at that time did not give general law cities the power to close streets permanently, and the City of Dublin was a general law city. Of course, general law cities have that authority now if they have the consent of all abutters.[100]

---

[99] *Id.* at 191.
[100] Tex. Transp. Code Ann. § 311.008 (West 2013).

Undeterred from closing streets, the City of Dublin tried again. In *City of Dublin v. Barrett*,[101] several citizens sued over the city's closure of the portion of a street at a railroad crossing. The closed segment had been used to cross the railroad tracks for over 20 years. As in the previous case, the city claimed the closure was for the protection of children. The court referred to the earlier case in which the same argument had failed and set the closure aside, finding that the closure was less about the children and more about the convenience and benefit of the railroad.

8.02.02. Need for Consent of Abutters.

General law cities need the consent of all abutting owners before closing a street.[102] Home-rule cities, in contrast, have the power to close streets without that consent.[103] Despite that difference, for their own protection, even home-rule cities should require consent from owners whose property abuts the segment to be closed. If a home-rule city forgoes that consent, it may be subject to injunction and perhaps a damage claim.[104]

8.02.03. Unanimity Requirement.

Consent of abutters means unanimous consent of abutters. The statute affords relief to any non-consenting abutter, so a majority of the abutting owners cannot bind a dissenting minority. That is so even though developers often would like you to believe otherwise.

---

[101] 242 S.W. 535 (Tex. Civ. App.—San Antonio 1922, writ dism'd w.o.j.).

[102] Tex. Transp. Code Ann. § 311.008 (West 2013).

[103] *Id.* § 311.007.

[104] Tex. Civ. Prac. & Rem. Code Ann. § 65.015 (West 2008).

The more owners whose consent is necessary, the less likely it is that consent will be unanimous. If you handle street closures, you will almost certainly encounter someone who has all consents except for one or two holdouts. The would-be street closer will be incredulous that the matter can't be settled by majority vote. But owners have a property interest in the streets in their subdivision. A majority of your neighbors cannot vote to divest you of your property.

As onerous as the unanimity requirement may seem, the law is equally onerous on owners whose property abuts the same street but does not abut the segment being closed. The City of Denton closed a street, and Caldwell and Hunt sued to set the closure aside, alleging that two of the council members voting for the closure had an improper interest in the outcome. In *Caldwell v. City of Denton*,[105] the court found that the possible improper interest of council members was irrelevant, because neither Caldwell nor Hunt owned property abutting the segment that was closed.

8.02.04. Forgoing Consent to Facilitate Projects.

Home-rule cities have the power to forgo consent,[106] and they may wish to do so when unanimous consent cannot be obtained for a city project. In such cases, a home-rule city's assumption of litigative risk is merely another cost of its project. But most often the lack of unanimous consent arises with private applicants, and municipal officials have to weigh the propriety of taxpayers assuming litigative risk in aid of a private project. Economic

---

[105] 556 S.W.2d 107 (Tex. Civ. App.—Fort Worth 1977, writ ref'd n.r.e.).
[106] Tex. Transp. Code Ann. § 311.007 (West 2013).

development officials will always vigorously assert the benefits of a given project, but they will leave it to the City Attorney to explain to council why the city got sued by trying to help a private developer.

8.02.05. Abutting at a Dead End.

An abutting owner may be one whose property abuts only at a dead end. In *Town of Palm Valley v. Johnson*,[107] Johnson owned 25 acres outside of, but immediately abutting, the southern boundary of the Town of Palm Valley. Lemon Drive ran from the north to the town's southern boundary line, and the town's southern boundary was Johnson's northern boundary. Johnson wanted to subdivide his property and asked the Town of Palm Valley to allow him to extend Lemon Drive into his proposed subdivision. The town replatted Lemon Drive, removing the last four feet and cutting Johnson off from access. Johnson sued, and the court found him to be an abutter within the meaning of the statute giving a cause of action to abutters.[108] The court found the closure of the four-foot segment of Lemon Drive void for want of Johnson's consent.[109]

The Town of Palm Valley had a population of 1,304 in the 2010 census. To be home rule, a city must have a population of more than

---

[107] 17 S.W.3d 281 (Tex. App.—Corpus Christi 2000), *pet. denied*, 87 S.W.3d 110 (Tex. 2001). In denying petition, the Supreme Court nevertheless noted that, even under the facts presented, an applicant for an injunction must prove the same equitable grounds as applicants for other injunctions. 87 S.W.3d at 111.

[108] Tex. Civ. Prac. & Rem. Code Ann. § 65.015 (West 2008).

[109] 17 S.W.3d at 287.

5,000.[110] Therefore, the Town of Palm Valley is almost certainly a general law city, which needs consent of all abutters to close a street.[111]

8.02.06. *Circuity of Travel.*

Persons whose property does not abut a closure but who nevertheless are inconvenienced by it are less fortunate than non-consenting abutters. They are not entitled to compensation merely because they and their customers must travel a more circuitous route after closure. In 1969, the City of San Antonio closed an alley, thereby benefiting First National Bank but injuring nearby owners. In *City of San Antonio v. Olivares,*[112] the injured owners sought compensation for impaired access to their hotel. The injured owners lost because they were not in the same block as the segment closed and still had remaining, albeit less convenient, access to their property.

That circuity or inconvenience of travel is not compensable was reaffirmed in *Milwee-Jackson Joint Venture v. Dallas Area Rapid Transit.*[113] A property owner was not entitled to compensation even though its only access was by means of an ingress-egress easement through a flood plain.

---

[110] Tex. Const. art. XI, § 5; Tex. Loc. Gov't Code Ann. § 9.001 (West Supp. 2013).

[111] Tex. Transp. Code Ann. § 311.008 (West 2013).

[112] 505 S.W.2d 526 (Tex. 1974).

[113] 350 S.W.3d 772 (Tex. App.—Dallas 2011, no pet.).

8.02.07. Statute of Limitations to Assert Wrongful Street Closure.

One aggrieved by an improper street closure must assert the cause of action within two years.[114]

8.02.08. Creation of Dead Ends.

The problem of dead ends often arises when closing segments of streets. Most planners do not like dead ends. Dead ends impair connectivity and emergency response times. Especially if a dead-end street does not have a cul-de-sac, a fire truck or other large vehicle may be significantly slowed if it turns onto it by mistake.

On the other hand, if a dead end already exists, moving the dead end forward by closing some part of the end of the street is often not a problem. Streets making a dead end at railroad tracks, drainage ways, and freeways without frontage roads are possible examples. Abutters must agree to the closure, but often the request is made by one who owns all the property at the end of the street.

Creating a dead end may be mitigated by requiring either a cul-de-sac or, depending on street patterns, an alternate connection to a nearby street. Either option may adequately solve the problem created by a dead end, but both options are often resisted because of expense. Those making policy decisions will have to weigh connectivity and safety against facilitating a developer's project.

---

[114] Tex. Civ. Prac. & Rem. Code Ann. § 16.005 (West 2002).

8.02.09. Do You Need to Deliver a Deed When Closing a Street?

Not if the street exists by easement. No one would deliver a deed when releasing a private ingress-egress easement, and there is no reason to treat a public street right-of-way easement differently.

For those occasions when giving a deed cannot be avoided, a sample form for a deed is attached as **Sample B**. If the city owned the street in fee, the form will need editing, because it refers to an easement and because it is a quitclaim deed, which cannot support a chain of title.

The attached sample does not name a grantee. Ownership of the fee underlying the street easement already exists, and no deed given in connection with a closure should cloud that title. Ascertaining who the grantee should be often raises title issues unnecessarily difficult to resolve in a street closure. Unless the city requires a title commitment for the entire closed segment, a simple solution is to provide that the title to the underlying fee goes to the owners of the underlying fee as their interests may appear.

If the city owns the street in fee, the issues are different. In those cases, closing the street takes away the state's street right-of-way easement, but it does not deprive the city of its fee ownership. In such cases, the fee should be disposed of according to law.

The purchaser of a closed street segment will often be an abutting owner. There's no legal requirement that it be so, but as we've seen above, even home-rule cities are well advised to assure that abutting owners consent to closure. In many cases, it would be difficult to get that consent if the city proposes to sell the segment to someone else.

8.02.10. What Issues Should a Street Closure Ordinance Address?

A street closure ordinance should set out background facts to bolster the public purpose behind the closure. Possible such facts might be that the subject segment is unimproved and unused, that the segment had not been maintained by the city, or that the segment is not regularly used as a path of travel. In such cases, relieving the city of the obligation to maintain the segment may contribute to a public purpose. Frequent dumping may be another justification.

The ordinance should specify what rights are affected by the closure. Consider limiting the ordinance's effect to removing the public's right to travel and perhaps removing the right to install new utility facilities. If utilities have to remove existing facilities in the segment to be closed, they may come to the city looking for reimbursement.

When redevelopment requires moving utilities, the cost of relocation must be borne by somebody. Why should the taxpayers or the utility ratepayers bear the expense for the benefit of the person performing the redevelopment? Better that the redeveloper bears the expense. The redeveloper is best situated to spread the expense over the ultimate users.

Consider also the possibility that the city has rights in the affected segment arising other than because the area is a street. Though unlikely, it is not impossible, and neither the lawyer drafting the closure ordinance nor the staff with whom the lawyer works is likely to know of these rights. For that reason, it is good to state that the ordinance does not release rights arising other than from the plat or other instrument creating the street.

The ordinance should, of course, also identify the segment to be closed, preferably by metes and bounds. Identifying abutting owners and their properties may help the county clerk's office index the ordinance properly when recorded. If a street closure ordinance is not properly indexed in the deed records, subsequent purchasers will not acquire actual notice of the closure and any reservations from the closure, such as the right of existing utilities to remain.

Subsequent purchasers without actual notice of reservations from closures will likely have constructive notice of them, so they probably have no legal redress. But such purchasers may take their case to elected officials, pleading unfairness. Pleas in that forum may often be successful. Whatever you can do to increase the odds of actual notice is worth the effort.

If the segment being closed exists by easement, as most streets do, then it is helpful to state that explicitly. Point out that the fee ownership under the street easement pre-existed the closure and is unaffected by it, except that, because of the closure, the fee interest is unburdened to the extent street easement rights are released.

If the segment is owned in fee, closing the street does not *ipso facto* entitle the city to convey the former street. A city could if it wished close a fee-owned street and retain use of the former street for some other purpose. If the city wants to convey the fee to the person requesting the street closure, ordinary property disposition procedures apply. Fortunately for those requesting closure of fee streets, the Local Government Code offers an exception to the usual notice and bidding requirements applicable to city property generally.[115] There is no exception, however, to the statutory and constitutional requirements to get fair market value.[116] That is seldom a popular answer.

A draft street closure ordinance appears at **Sample C.**

8.03. Can Cities Allow Non-Street Uses by Abutting Owners?

8.03.01. Chapter 316.

Chapter 316 of the Transportation Code is the starting point for determining permissibility of encroachments on a public street. The chapter has two parts: Subchapter A governs public conveniences and amenities, and Subchapter B governs private uses. Subchapter A's rules for public conveniences and amenities consist of multiple sections and set out detailed requirements. Paradoxically, Subchapter B's rules for private uses consist of only one subsection and set out a comparatively loose standard. That is the reverse of how one might expect the difference to fall.

8.03.02. Public Conveniences and Amenities.

The permissible right-of-way encroachments for public conveniences and amenities are: (1) trees or decorative landscaping, including landscaping lighting, watering systems, or other

---

[115] *Id.* § 272.001(b)(2).

[116] *Id.* § 272.001(b); Tex. Const. art. 11, § 3.

accessories; (2) sidewalk cafes; (3) ornamental gates, columns, or other ornamental works marking neighborhood entrances; (4) supportive or decorative columns, arches, or other structural or decorative features meeting certain criteria; and (5) other public amenities such as transit bus shelters, drinking fountains, and benches. Permits may be given only to the fee owner, a lessee, or someone with written permission from the fee owner.[117]

The city council or a designated city official must support issuance of each permit by specific findings: (1) the improvement or facility will not be located on, extend onto, or intrude on the roadway; or a part of the sidewalk needed for pedestrian use; (2) the improvement or facility will not create a hazardous condition or obstruction of vehicular or pedestrian travel on the municipal street; and (3) the design and location of the improvement or facility includes all reasonable planning to minimize potential injury or interference to the public in the use of the municipal street.[118] The statute sets out detailed requirements for a permit system, should a city want to adopt one.[119]

8.03.03. Private Uses.

In addition to public conveniences and amenities, a city may permit a private use of the public right-of-way if the use does not: (1) interfere with the public use of the street or sidewalk, or (2) create a dangerous condition on the street or sidewalk.[120]

---

[117] Tex. Transp. Code Ann. § 316.002 (West 2013).
[118] *Id.* § 316.003.
[119] *Id.* § 316.004.
[120] *Id.* § 316.021.

Courts have addressed many private uses of public right-of-way to determine whether the private use interferes with the public use.

8.03.03. A. Private Uses That Do Not Interfere with Public's Use of the Streets.

Recall the general principle that abutting owners own the fee under street easements to the middle of the street. That ownership allows abutting owners to use the street in ways that do not interfere with the public's use. For example, the City of Fort Worth charged rent to a hotel for a basement that extended under the public sidewalk. At one time, deliveries were commonly made to downtown buildings through their basements. Many basements extended under the sidewalks and were accessed by means of stairs or an elevator from the sidewalks. Sidewalks next to older buildings to this day often have doors down to basements.

In *Citizen's Hotel v. City of Fort Worth*,[121] the court noted several material points: (1) the city held the streets not in a proprietary capacity but as a trustee for the public, (2) the hotel's use did not interfere with any existing public use, (3) the proposed charge was neither a tax nor related to any problem the hotel was causing, (4) the city had no plans to devote to public use the area occupied by the basement, (5) the hotel owner conceded that the city could take the area whenever it was needed for public use, and (6) the proposed charge was not related to any cost to the city for licensing or policing the area.[122]

---

[121] 380 S.W.2d 60 (Tex. Civ. App—Fort Worth 1964, writ ref'd n.r.e.).
[122] *Id.* at 61.

Under the facts found in that case, the court enjoined the City of Fort Worth's attempt to impose the charge. That was in part because the hotel was using its own property. It owned the fee under street easement. Given that the hotel was not interfering with public use of the streets, it was entitled to continue to use its basement.

State v. Dunn[123] is discussed in Section 7.07.04 (Flexible Rights for Future Work), but it is germane here as well. As noted, Dunn owed two tracts. The tracts were divided by U.S. 87 and a railroad right-of-way. Dunn ran an irrigation pipe between the two properties, underneath the two intervening rights-of-way. The well feeding the irrigation system was on the tract the state was condemning to build Interstate 27.

The state contested Dunn's claim of damages for loss of the well, arguing that Dunn did not have a right to run the pipes under the existing highway. But because Dunn owned the fee under part of the highway and had a water-pipeline easement for the rest, he succeeded in his claim.

Dunn's water line under the highway and railroad tracks was permissible because he owned the property rights necessary to run the line and because his exercise of those rights did not interfere with either the highway or the railroad. It became a problem only when the state condemned additional rights from him.

A city may find it useful to require a registration, licensing, or permit system for all permissible encroachments. In so doing, the fee should not exceed that allowed by point six in the court's discussion in *Citizen's Hotel v. City of Fort Worth,* and the city

---

[123] 574 S.W.2d 821 (Tex. Civ. App.—Amarillo 1978, writ ref'd n.r.e.).

should be mindful of the limitations and requirements of Chapter 316 of the Texas Transportation Code.

8.03.03 B. Private Uses That Interfere with Public's Use of the Streets.

As previously discussed, the city holds no proprietary right in the streets but rather administers them in trust for the public. Paragraph 8.02.01 shows that, as a consequence of that trust, street closures must be supported by a public purpose. Encroachments onto public streets invoke the same principles. Further, private uses that interfere with public use violate the Transportation Code.[124]

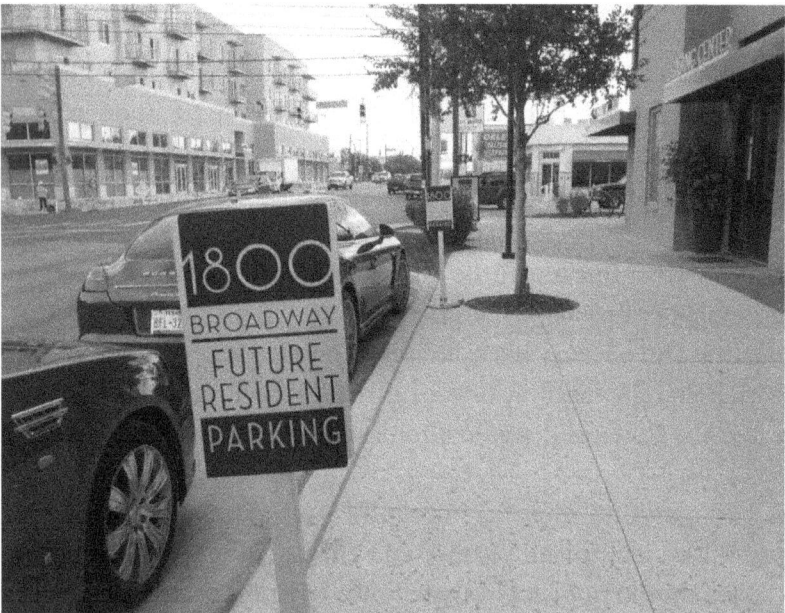

---

[124] Tex. Transp. Code Ann. § 316.021 (West 2013).

An example of interference with public use of streets is a property owner claiming private on-street parking rights. Parking is a legitimate public use of the streets where not otherwise prohibited. Excluding the public from parking to give preference to a private owner seems a per se interference with public use and is difficult to square with municipalities' public trust. The tree shown in the nearby photograph falls squarely into the public amenity category. That is in contrast to the private-parking signs, which are almost certainly beyond the power of a city to authorize, because they grant a private right in violation of the public trust.

8.03.04. Limitations Claims Against Streets.

No matter how long an abutting owner or someone else occupies a street segment or otherwise uses it adversely to street uses, a city will not lose title to the street by adverse possession.[125]

8.04. Can Cities Allow Non-Street Uses by Non-Abutting Owners?

Transportation Code Sec. 316 limits public-convenience-and-amenity encroachments to fee owners, lessees, or those with written permission from the fee owner.126 Private uses, however, are not limited in the same way. Part of the answer for private uses lies in the ownership interests in the street.

---

[125] Tex. Civ. Prac. & Rem. Code Ann. § 16.061 (West 2008).
[126] Tex. Transp. Code Ann. § 316.002(b) (West 2013).

For easement streets, under simple principles of property law, cities lack the power to consent to anyone other than the abutting owner using street easement right-of-way for non-street-related uses. Street-related uses are all the rights the city has. The rest of the rights remain with the owner of the underlying fee.

For example, in *Hale County v. Davis*,[127] a property owner C needed water and reached a deal with A, who had water to spare. A got permission from Hale County to run a private water line down the county road from his land to C's land, but the water line had to pass by B's land. B objected and succeeded in preventing the line. Hale County did not have the power to authorize a private water line in the public road over B's objection, because a private water line is not a street-related use.

The result of *Hale County v. Davis* flows from the owner of the fee retaining rights to use the right-of-way for so long as those uses do not interfere with public use. Public uses of the right-of-way are so broad that this issue does not come up often. But it came up in *Hale County v. Davis*, and it can arise when a city is willing to permit a private use but only for a significant fee. How can a city charge a fee for permitting a trespass on another's property?

The result in Hale County would have been different had A been a certificated water utility, which is demonstrated by *Blackburn v. Brazos County Utilities, Inc.*[128] Property owners sued for trespass because of a water line installed in the road in front of their home.

---

[127] *Hale Cnty. v. Davis*, 572 S.W.2d 63 (Tex. Civ. App.—Amarillo 1978, writ ref'd n.r.e.).
[128] 777 S.W.2d 758 (Tex. App.—Beaumont 1989, writ denied).

But in this case, the entity installing the line was a public utility and, accordingly, had a right to lay its lines in public streets.

Marcus Cable Associates, L.P. v. Krohn[129] arose from a television cable company wanting to put its cable in an easement the fee owner had granted to Hill Country Electric for the purpose of constructing and maintaining an electric transmission or distribution line or system. The Texas Supreme Court found that laying television cable was outside the scope of rights granted. Thus the fee owner had not consented to cable television lines. Because the trial court had ruled for the cable company without trial, the Supreme Court remanded the case for trial.

Though *Marcus Cable* concerned a private electric easement and not a public street, both are easements. While the permissible uses of an electric easement are different from the permissible uses of a public street, to determine whether a given use is permissible, the question in both cases is whether the proposed use exceeds the permissible scope of use.

In *City of San Antonio v. Rische*,[130] the plaintiff sought to enjoin construction and operation of a rail line running along Jones Street eastward from the Lone Star Brewery to the Galveston, Harrisburg, and San Antonio Railway (now Union Pacific) tracks. The plaintiff alleged that the tracks were for a purely private purpose. The court of civil appeals noted that, to be valid, grants of rights to use public streets must be public. Streets are held in trust

---

[129] 90 S.W.3d 697 (Tex. 2002).
[130] 38 S.W. 388 (Tex. Civ. App.—San Antonio 1896, writ ref'd).

for public purposes "and no other."[131] The court went on to note that the council's action in granting the railroad use was "without semblance of authority," and the tracks were a "nuisance hurtful to the public."[132] The trial court had enjoined construction of the tracks, and the court of civil appeals affirmed.

Cities may be asked to allow private pipelines down their streets. Given that private pipelines are not within the city's easement rights, all a city can do is set the conditions under which the pipeline, if installed, would not interfere with the public's use of the streets.

The pipeline installer must then acquire private pipeline rights from the fee owners of all the parcels by which the pipeline passes. The same principle applies when the water and sewer utility wants to place water or sewer lines along a drainage easement. Water and sewer lines are not among the rights taken for a drainage easement. As a result, the city's role is to assure that the water and sewer lines do not interfere with drainage. The water and sewer utility must get the necessary rights from the owners of affected fee.

Pipelines buried in the street do not present the same problem as the rail lines in *City of San Antonio v. Rische*. That is because, unlike railroad tracks, once a pipeline is buried it will not interfere with traffic.

---

[131] *Id.* at 390.
[132] *Id.*

8.05. Sample Joint-Use Agreement.

A sample joint-use agreement for use of street right-of-way or other easements is attached at Sample D.

———

9. Parking.

9.01. General Rule.

L ocal authorities are specifically authorized by statute to regulate stopping, standing, or parking on highways.[133] Cities are included in the definition of "local authorities,"[134] and "highways" means the width between the boundary lines of a publicly maintained way, any part of which is open to the public for vehicular travel.[135] Accordingly, for the purposes of this statute, highways include streets.

9.02. Privileged Parking.

The legal rules governing who gets to park for free where and for how long bring to mind Sayre's Law: In any dispute, the intensity of feeling is inversely proportional to the value of the issues at

---

[133] Tex. Transp. Code Ann. § 542.202(a)(2) (West 2013).

[134] *Id.* § 541.002(3).

[135] *d.* § 541.302(5).

stake.[136] A similar paradox exists as to complexity of the rules. One expects complexity in the securities laws and the Internal Revenue Code. One might be surprised about parking rules.

The rules are a mixture of state law and local ordinances. Local ordinances vary, and this handbook does not undertake an examination of the rules for every city in Texas. The State of Texas and City of San Antonio rules are summarized as follows:

City Garages:

1. Disabled with placard or license plate[137] or bearing the international symbol of access issued by a state or a state or province of a foreign country.	Unlimited parking in spaces marked for the disabled, but not otherwise privileged.[138, 139]
2. Persons issued Disabled Veterans plate.	Unlimited parking in spaces marked for the disabled, but not otherwise privileged.[140, 141]

---

[136] *Sayre's Law*, Wikipedia, https://en.wikipedia.org/wiki/Sayre%27s_Law (last modified Oct. 16, 2013).

[137] Assuming they are displayed according to legal requirements.

[138] Tex. Transp. Code Ann. § 681.006(a) (West 2013).

[139] This does not permit parking at a time when or place where parking is prohibited.

[140] Tex. Transp. Code Ann. §§ 504.202(a), 681.008(a) (West Supp. 2013).

[141] This does not permit parking at a time when or place where parking is prohibited.

3. Military Honor Plates.

a. Persons issued POW or Purple Heart Plates.	Exempt from payment of parking fees collected at parking garages that are owned or leased by the city.[142, 143]
b. Other Military Honor Plates.	No special privileges at City garages.

City Parking Lots

1. Disabled with placard or license plate[144] or bearing the international symbol of access issued by a state or a state or province of a foreign country.	Unlimited parking in spaces marked for the disabled, but not otherwise privileged.[145, 146]
2. Persons issued Disabled Veterans plate.	Unlimited parking in spaces marked for the disabled, but not otherwise privileged.[147, 148]

---

[142] San Antonio, Tex., Code of Ordinances § 19-210 (1986).

[143] This does not permit parking at a time when or place where parking is prohibited.

[144] Assuming they are displayed according to legal requirements.

[145] Tex. Transp. Code Ann. § 681.006(a) (West 2013).

[146] This does not permit parking at a time when or place where parking is prohibited.

[147] Tex. Transp. Code §§ 504.202(a), 681.008(a) (West Supp. 2013).

[148] This does not permit parking at a time when or place where parking is prohibited.

3. Military Honor Plates.

a. Persons issued POW or Purple Heart Plates. — Exempt from payment of parking fees collected at parking lots that are owned or leased by the city.[149]

b. Other Military Honor Plates. — No special privileges at City parking lots.

Parking Meters

1. Disabled with placard or license plate[150] or bearing the international symbol of access issued by a state or a state or province of a foreign country. — No fee when parking at a meter. Because this section does not ban penalties, persons with this privilege must comply with meter time limits.[151, 152, 153]

---

[149] San Antonio, Tex., Code of Ordinances § 19-210 (1986).

[150] Assuming they are displayed according to legal requirements.

[151] Tex. Transp. Code Ann. § 681.006(b) (West 2013).

[152] OAG H-1291.

[153] This does not permit parking at a time when or place where parking is prohibited.

2.	Persons issued Disabled Veterans plate.	No fee when parking at a meter. Because this section does not ban penalties, persons with this privilege must comply with meter time limits.[154, 155, 156]
3.	Persons issued POW plates, persons issued Pearl Harbor Survivor plates, recipients of the Congressional Medal of Honor, and recipients of the Purple Heart.	No fee when parking at a meter. Because this section does not ban penalties, persons with this privilege must comply with meter time limits.[157, 158, 159, 160]

The above rules do not generally apply to the federal government or to airports.

9.03. Residential Parking Permits.

In residential areas near downtowns or near other areas attracting parking by those who are neither residents nor invitees of residents, outside parkers may dominate street parking. In such cases,

[154] Tex. Transportation Code § 681.008(b), §§ 504.202(a), 504.315(c), (d), (e), and (g).

[155] OAG H-1291.

[156] This does not permit parking at a time when or place where parking is prohibited.

[157] Tex. Transp. Code Ann. § 681.008(b) (West 2013), §§ 504.202(a), 504.315(c)–(e), (g) (West Supp. 2013).

[158] San Antonio, Tex., Code of Ordinances § 19-210 (1986).

[159] OAG H-1291.

[160] 434 U.S. 5 (1977).

the interests of the residents will generally be more concentrated than the interests of the outside parkers, so the residents may succeed in persuading politicians to give residents preferential or exclusive parking rights.

In *County Board of Arlington County, Virginia v. Richards*,[161] the U.S. Supreme Court rejected an equal protection challenge against the resident-only parking permit system of Arlington County, Virginia. The challenged ordinance directed the county manager to determine which neighborhoods were especially crowded by parking from outside the neighborhood and to establish a permit system in those neighborhoods. The court applied the rational-basis standard to the discrimination between residents and nonresidents and found that abatement of air pollution and other adverse environmental effects of commuting justified the discrimination.

Cities wishing to avail themselves of the benefit of *County Board of Arlington County, Virginia v. Richards* may wish to structure their programs so they can colorably claim the same goals the Supreme Court found sufficient in that case. But even if a city does not so structure its program, it is difficult to lose a case under a rational-basis review, so it is possible another rationale would be upheld.

Do not overlook, however, that a Fourteenth Amendment equal-protection challenge is all that *County Board of Arlington County, Virginia v. Richards* considered. That case arose in Virginia rather than Texas, and the court did not address a challenge mounted under any aspect of Texas state law. Favoring one class of citizens

---

[161] 434 U.S. 5 (1977).

over others in doling out public rights may not be an equal-protection violation, but it is hard to reconcile with the public trust that Texas law imposes on cities' management of the streets.

There are many reported cases in which cities have elevated private interests over the public interest in streets. Cities have lost many of those cases. For example, in the 1920s, the Radford Grocery Store in Abilene loaded and unloaded merchandise by means of a platform that extended from the building to the curb. Several other businesses had similar platforms up and down the street. The City of Abilene decided that it wanted the platforms removed. In *J.M. Radford Grocery Co. v. City of Abilene*,[162] the grocery store owner defended in part by showing that the Abilene City Council had authorized his platform in 1905. But the court found that the city lacked the power to surrender its authority over any portion of the street or to authorize a permanent appropriation of part of the street to a private use.

In *City of San Antonio v. Rische*,[163] the plaintiff sought to enjoin construction and operation of the rail line running along Jones Street eastward from the Lone Star Brewery to the Galveston, Harrisburg, and San Antonio Railway (now Union Pacific) tracks. The plaintiff alleged and the trial court found that the tracks were for a purely private purpose. The court of civil appeals noted that, to be valid, grants of rights to use public streets must be public—that is, that streets are held in trust for public purposes "and no other."[164] The court went on to note that the council's action in

---

[162] 34 S.W.2d 830 (Tex. Comm'n App. 1931, judgm't adopted).
[163] 38 S.W. 388 (Tex. Civ. App.—San Antonio 1896, writ ref'd).
[164] *Id.* at 390.

granting the railroad use was "without semblance of authority" and that the tracks were a "nuisance hurtful to the public."[165] The trial court had enjoined construction of the tracks, and the court of civil appeals affirmed.

In *Kalteyer v. Sullivan*,[166] the San Antonio City Council authorized Mr. Sullivan to obstruct an alley with gates and to store building material in the alley. The court set aside the City Council action favoring Sullivan. In so doing, the court opined that the public should not have "to expect their trustees to become aiders and abettors of an individual in excluding them from and depriving them of the use of their highways." Rather, the public should be able to look to the council for protection from such things.[167]

In *Texas Co. v. Texarkana Machine Shops*,[168] a private party sued other private parties, seeking removal of obstructions in a street. The obstructions had been placed after the City of Texarkana had closed, vacated, and abandoned the street. The trial court enjoined the obstruction, and the court of civil appeals affirmed, noting the public trust character of the street.[169]

A physical platform as in *J.M. Radford Grocery* or the interruption to traffic by a railroad as in *Rische* are greater appropriations of the public street for a private purpose than granting special parking privileges, but the special privileges are themselves a form of private appropriation. The street closings in *Kalteyer* and *Texarkana*

---

[165] *Id.*

[166] 18 Tex. Civ. App. 488, 46 S.W. 288 (San Antonio 1898, writ ref'd).

[167] *Id.* at 494, 46 S.W. at 290.

[168] 1 S.W.2d 928 (Tex. Civ. App.—Texarkana 1928, no writ).

[169] *Id.* at 931.

Machine Shops were likewise greater appropriation than would be special parking privileges.

But since each of the merchants owned the fee under the street easement, no other members of the public likely had a claim of right to install a platform in place of those installed by the merchants in *J.M. Radford Grocery*. In contrast, every member of the public has a claim of right to park in the area for which special parking rights may be set aside. Members of the public would be more adversely affected than they were in *J.M. Radford Grocery*.

The question becomes one of degree and balancing. Without Texas authority on point, it is difficult to predict what a court might do. That plans such as this exist in various Texas cities and have been found to be proper in other states may persuade a court to uphold the program. Or it may not.

The public trust aspect of streets is discussed extensively in Section 8 (Are Cities Free to Do Anything They Want With Public Streets?).

———

10. Texas Department of Transportation Turnback Program.

10.01. TxDOT's Budget Cut.

Most Texas municipal lawyers are probably aware that the 2013 legislature told TxDOT to reduce spending. To comply, TxDOT is turning over maintenance of many state highways located within city limits to cities of at least 50,000 in population.

10.02. Distinction Between City Streets and State Highways Within City Limits.

How TxDOT can do this is tied to the distinction between city streets and state highways. Home-rule cities have exclusive control of streets within their limits and may (1) control, regulate, or remove an encroachment or obstruction on a public street or alley of the city; (2) open or change a public street or alley of the city; or (3) improve a public highway, street, or alley of the city.[170] Correspondingly, TxDOT has exclusive and direct control of improvement of the state highway system.[171] Whether a highway is part of the state highway system is up to the Transportation Commission so that the commission has the power to remove a highway from the state system.[172]

Thus, cities control all streets within their limits except, arguably, streets that are part of the state highway system. And the Transportation Commission has the power to remove streets from the state highway system. So if the commission removes a street from the system, then the city in which the street is located is on the hook for maintenance of the street, regardless of who owns the fee. In practice, however, TxDOT takes the position that cities are responsible for all streets within their corporate limits except for those streets for which the city and TxDOT have entered into a municipal maintenance agreement.

10.03. Agreements Between TxDOT and Municipalities.

Municipal maintenance agreements may (1) provide for the location, relocation, improvement, control, supervision, and regulation of a designated state highway in the municipality; and (2) establish the respective liabilities and responsibilities of the commission and the municipality under the agreement.[173] TxDOT

---

[170] Tex. Transp. Code Ann. § 311.001 (West 2013).

[171] *Id.* § 224.031 (West 2011).

[172] *Id.* § 201.103 (West Supp. 2013).

[173] *Id.* § 221.002 (West 2011).

often uses such agreements to allocate responsibilities within municipalities.

Whether the Transportation Commission unilaterally removes a highway from the state highway system or whether TxDOT refuses to enter into a municipal maintenance agreement as to a given highway, TxDOT and the Transportation Commission hold the legal cards regarding maintenance of state highways within a city's corporate limits. The only check on their discretion is whether their actions pass muster with the legislative committees having oversight.

10.04. Irrelevance of "Ownership" of the Highways.

When considering this problem, some may focus on whether the state or the city owns the streets. And it is true that, despite the arguments presented under Section 7 (Should Street Right-of-Way be Purchased in Fee or by Easement?), TxDOT's current practice is to buy right-of-way in fee. But the statutes cited above, which control who maintains what right-of-way, do not address ownership of the fee. Bear that in mind if TxDOT tries to slough the fee off on your city.

10.05. Refusal to Accept Deed.

If TxDOT is turning over maintenance of a highway segment to a city and holds the fee to the segment, it may want the city to accept a deed to the fee. A city's acceptance of the fee conveyance would relieve TxDOT of the associated liabilities discussed in

Sections 7.01 through 7.05. But ownership of the fee under the street is irrelevant to who maintains the street.

TxDOT voluntarily chose to assume the liabilities of fee owner-ship. The city may have to accept maintenance, but it doesn't have to accept conveyance of the fee. After all, the fee under most city streets is owned to the centerline by the owners of the abutting property.[174] See Section 2 (Who Owns the Streets?). Cities never-theless maintain those streets. Nothing impairs a city's ability to maintain a street when the state owns the underlying fee.

A deed from the state to the city for fee ownership under the street is all the more peculiar given that the right-of-way interest itself would remain with the state.[175] See Section 2 (Who Owns the Streets?). So the state's transfer to a city of the fee under the right-of-way is all the more transparently an effort to shift ancil-lary liability to the city.

A city's acceptance of the fee under a former state highway may be compelled by political considerations, but it is not compelled or even desirable by legal ones.

———

[174] *Miller v. Cretien*, 488 S.W.2d 893, 896–97 (Tex. Civ. App.—Fort Worth, 1972, writ ref'd n.r.e.).

[175] *Texas Dep't of Transp. v. City of Sunset Valley*, 146 S.W.3d 637, 644 (Tex. 2004); *West v. City of Waco*, 294 S.W. 832 (Tex. 1927).

Sample A: Public-Street Easement Deed

Notice of Confidentiality Rights: If You Are a Natural Person, You May Remove or Strike Any or All the Following Information from Any Instrument That Transfers an Interest in Real Property Before it Is Filed for Record in the Public Records: Your Social Security Number or Your Driver's License Number.

State of Texas   §
                        §   **Know All By These Presents:**
County of ??? §

Public-Street-Easement Deed

Ordinance Authorizing Acceptance:	
Grantor:	???
Grantor's Address:	???
Grantee:	City of ????
Grantee's Address:	???
Purpose of Easement:	Public street right-of-way purposes, allowing all rights incident to public streets or alleys.

Property: /?????/, the land being more particularly described on **Exhibit A**, which is incorporated by reference for all purposes as if fully set forth.

Consideration: $XXX — or — The benefits accruing to Grantor, to Grantor's other property, and to the public

Grantor grants and conveys to Grantee and to the public generally, for the Consideration, an easement in gross, in perpetuity over, across, under, and upon the Property for the Purpose of Easement. Grantee may (A) construct, maintain, reconstruct, remove, relocate, and replace improvements related to the Purpose of Easement anywhere within the Property; (B) may inspect, patrol, and police the Property; (C) may remove all trees and other vegetation and all other natural or artificial obstructions from the Property; and (D) may further excavate, fill, level, grade, pave, and otherwise improve the Property as may be conducive to the Purpose of Easement. Delineation of these powers does not impair other powers and uses otherwise incident to public street right-of-way. This instrument burdens the Property to the same extent as if it were a platted street or alley. Grantor covenants for itself, its heirs, executors, successors, and assigns that no permanent building or obstruction of any kind will be placed on the Property.

To Have and To Hold the above described easement and rights unto the public until its use is abandoned.

Grantor binds itself and its heirs, executors, successors, and assigns, to warrant and forever defend, all and singular, the above described easement and rights unto Grantee and the public against every person whomsoever lawfully claiming or to claim the same or any part thereof. This easement is assignable to any governmental entity having jurisdiction over the public streets in the area in which the Property is located.

In Witness Whereof, Grantor has caused it representative to set its hand, this _____ day of _____, 2013.

/signature block for grantor/

/acknowledgment for grantor/

Sample B: Street-Closure Deed

Notice of Confidentiality Rights: If You Are a Natural Person, You May Remove or Strike Any or All the Following Information from Any Instrument That Transfers an Interest in Real Property Before it Is Filed for Record in the Public Records: Your Social Security Number or Your Driver's License Number.

State of Texas   }
    }
County of ????}

Quitclaim Deed

Authorizing Ordinance:	
SP No./Parcel:	
Grantor:	City of ?????
Grantor's Mailing Address:	?????
Consideration:	$10 in hand paid and other good and valuable consideration, the receipt and adequacy of which are hereby acknowledged.

90

Property: All of the real property situated within the corporate limits of the City of ?????, described by metes and bounds **Exhibit A** attached hereto and incorporated herein verbatim for all purposes.

Grantor, for the Consideration, Quitclaims and Releases to the owners of the underlying fee, as their interests may appear, all of Grantor's right, title, interest, and estate, both at law and in equity, if any, as of the date hereof, in and to the Property, together with, all and singular, the rights and appurtenances thereto in anywise belonging.

Grantor does not warrant that it has any interest in the Property. Grantor names no specific grantees in this instrument, because it does not assume the burden of identifying the correct owners of the underlying fee.

This deed does not affect or impair any public rights in the subject tract for drainage, water and wastewater lines, electric transmission lines, communication lines of all types, or any other rights except for the right of the public to travel on the subject tract.

In Witness Whereof, Grantor has caused its representative to set its hand:

/signature block for grantor/

/acknowledgment for grantor/

Sample C: Street-Closure Ordinance

AN ORDINANCE

CLOSING, VACATING, AND ABANDONING A ???????

———

WHEREAS, the Right-of-Way Segment, as defined below, is/is not improved.

WHEREAS, the Right-of-Way Segment is/is not overgrown and subject to dumping.

WHEREAS, the Right-of-Way Segment is/is not being maintained by the City of San Antonio.

WHEREAS, the Right-of-Way Segment does/does not show signs of being used regularly as a path of travel.

WHEREAS, it is in the interests of the public that the City of San Antonio be relieved of the obligation maintain the Right-of-Way Segment.

NOW THEREFORE,

BE IT ORDAINED BY THE CITY COUNCIL OF THE CITY OF SAN ANTONIO:

SECTION 1. Subject to the reservation below, the City finds the following right-of-way ("Right-of-Way Segment") is no longer essential to the safe and efficient flow of traffic in the area in which the right-of-way is located. As an exercise of its discretion, the City Council closes, vacates, and abandons the Right-of-Way Segment. A condition of the closure, vacation, and abandonment is City's receipt of the fee set out below in the funding section of this Ordinance. The Right-of-Way Segment is identified below.

That portion of ??? described generally as extending ??? from the ??? right-of-way line of ????? to the ???? right-of-way line of ????? Road.

SECTION 2. A picture of the Right-of-Way Segment is set forth at **Attachment I**. The detailed description of the Right-of-Way Segment is set forth on **Attachment II**. Both Attachments I and II are incorporated into this ordinance for all purposes as if they were fully set forth. Attachment II controls over any discrepancy between it and Attachment I.

SECTION 3. The Right-of-Way Segment exists by virtue of ????/ subdivision plat recorded at //a conveyance instrument recorded at //// ????

SECTION 4. The properties abutting the Right-of-Way Segment are:

Address: Description: Owner Listed by County Appraisal District:

The listing above is made solely to facilitate indexing this Ordinance in the real property records. If the listing is inaccurate or not comprehensive, it does not affect the validity of the closure.

SECTION 5. All presently existing water and wastewater lines and facilities, electric transmission and distribution lines and facilities, gas lines and facilities, communication lines and facilities, or any other public utility lines and facilities, if any, may remain in place despite this Ordinance and may continue to be used, repaired, enlarged, and maintained in the ordinary course of business. Any person wanting removal of an existing utility line or facility must negotiate separately with the pertinent utility. Any person building on the Right-of-Way Segment without first reaching an agreement with a utility having lines or facilities in the segment does so at his own risk. After the date of this Ordinance, no utility may add additional utility lines or facilities in the Right-of-Way Segment based on a claim that the Right-of-Way Segment is public street right-of-way. All existing drainage rights in the Right-of-Way Segment are retained by the City. This closure does not give up any right arising other than from the plat or other instrument creating the public street or alley right-of-way. Neither does this Ordinance create new easement rights.

SECTION 6. The City Manager or her designee, severally, are authorized and directed to execute and deliver all documents and to do all other things conducive to reflect this closure, abandonment, and vacation.

SECTION 7. The Right-of-Way Segment exists by easement. The underlying fee ownership of the Right-of-Way Segment by the adjacent lot owners is now unburdened by the rights closed, vacated, and abandoned. For purposes of future conveyance and to better reflect their ownership generally, owners of the adjacent property should replat. No such replat impairs the rights retained by City above, unless in the course of replatting, the owner, at its own expense, otherwise provides for those rights according to platting rules of general applicability.

SECTION 8. ////financial language//////.

SECTION 9. This ordinance becomes effective 10 days after passage, unless it receives the eight votes requisite to immediate effectiveness under San Antonio Municipal Code § 1-15, in which case it becomes effective immediately.

PASSED AND APPROVED this ???? day of ??????? 2014.

Sample D: Joint-Use Agreement

Joint Use Agreement
(Easement ??????.)

1. Pertinent Information.

Authorizing Ordinance:	
City:	City of ?????
City's Address:	
Joint User:	?????
Joint User's Address:	
Term:	Indefinite duration subject to rights of termination set out in this agreement.
Premises:	
Scope of Permission:	Installation, construction, reconstruction, realignment, inspection, patrolling, operation, maintenance, repair, addition, removal and replacement of _____, including all facilities and appurtenances convenient to accomplishing the purpose, and additions and replacements thereto
Fee:	

2. Permission.

2.01. City acknowledges that Joint User's activities, if within the Scope of Permission and conforming to the terms and conditions of this Agreement, do not, as of the date of the City's execution of this Permission set forth below, unreasonably interfere with City's rights in the Premises. The Permission is non-exclusive. This instrument does not create an easement, but only a license defined by the terms of this instrument. City will coordinate with Joint User any access or use that could affect Joint User's infrastructure within the Premises.

2.02. This Permission does not exempt Joint User from rules of general applicability governing activities within the Scope of Permission or from getting permits required generally for activities within the Scope of Permission.

2.03. **The Permission granted by this instrument bears only upon such rights as City may have in the Premises. Persons other than City may have rights in some or all of the Premises. City does not give permission to trespass on or otherwise affect or impair others' rights.**

3. Construction, Maintenance, and Operations.

3.01. **Costs.** Joint User is solely responsible for all costs of construction, installation, repairs, maintenance, operation, and the like of any property placed by Joint User in the Premises.

3.02. **Installation and Maintenance.** All pipes must be buried to a depth satisfactory to City. In determining proper depth, City may consider expected future as well as present uses of the Premises. If another governmental or other regulatory body prescribes a depth, that depth will be satisfactory to the City. Joint User must maintain all improvements constructed or installed by Joint User. In so doing, Joint User must adhere to all applicable safety standards and must adhere to all applicable federal, state, or local laws, rules, or regulations. Without limiting the foregoing, Joint User must assure that nothing it does causes the Premises to fail to comply with any aspect of the Unified Development Code relating to drainage.

3.03. **No Power to Bind**. Joint User cannot bind or permit another to bind City for payment of money or for any other obligation.

3.04. **Contractors and Subcontractors**. Joint User must promptly pay anyone who could file a mechanics' or materialmen's lien on the Premises, unless there is a good faith dispute about the right to payment. If any such lien is filed, Joint User shall pay or bond around such claim within 30 days after Joint User's notice of the lien, failing which, City may treat it as an event of default and terminate this Permission as provided in Section 6 below entitled "Termination." Joint User remains obligated to clear the lien without cost to City even after termination.

3.05 **Restoration**. If Joint User buries any pipes, promptly upon covering the pipes, Joint User must restore the original contours and vegetation disturbed by the burial to a condition substantially equivalent to their pre-existing condition, substantial equivalence to be determined by City. If an area has a natural appearance, Joint User must restore that natural appearance unless City otherwise agrees in writing. City's determination of natural appearance controls.

4. Insurance.
///insert desired insurance requirements///

5. Indemnity.
5.01. These definitions apply to the indemnity provisions of this Contract:

5.01.01. "Indemnified Claims" mean all loss, cost, liability, or expense, directly or indirectly arising, in whole or in part, out of acts or omissions of any person other than an Indemnitee that give rise to assertions of Indemnitee liability under this Contract. A claim is an Indemnified Claim even if the person alleged to be at fault is not a party to this agreement. Indemnified Claims include attorneys' fees and court costs and include claims arising from property damage and from personal or bodily injury, including death. Indemnified Claims also include claims in which an Indemnitee shares liability with the Indemnitor.

5.01.02. "Indemnitees" means the City of ????? and its elected officials, officers, employees, agents, and other representatives, collectively, against whom an Indemnified Claim has been asserted.

5.01.03. "Indemnitor" means Joint User.

5.02. Indemnitor must indemnify Indemnitees, individually and collectively, from all Indemnified Claims.

5.03. If one or more Indemnitees are finally adjudged to be solely negligent, Indemnitor need not further indemnify the so-adjudged Indemnitees from liability arising from the Indemnitees' adjudicated share of liability. But despite allegations that one or more Indemnitees bear such fault, Indemnitor must nevertheless defend all Indemnitees until final adjudication and all appeals have been exhausted. An Indemnitee may but need not waive appeals. Indemnitor may not recover sums previously spent defending or otherwise indemnifying Indemnitees finally adjudged to bear fault outside the scope of this indemnity and must continue to indemnify other Indemnitees if claims are still asserted against them.

5.04. There are no third-party beneficiaries of this indemnity other than the category of people and entities included within the definition of Indemnitees.

5.05. Indemnitor must promptly advise the City of ????? in writing of any Indemnified Claim and must, at its own cost, investigate and defend the Indemnified Claim. Whether or not the City of ????? is an Indemnitee as to a particular Indemnified Claim, the City of ????? may require Indemnitor to replace the counsel Indemnitor has hired to defend Indemnitees. The City may also require Indemnitor to hire specific-named counsel for so long as the named counsel's hourly rates do not exceed the usual and customary charges for counsel handling sophisticated and complex litigation in the locale where the suit is pending. No such actions release or impair Indemnitor's obligations under this indemnity paragraph, including its obligation to pay for the counsel selected by City. Regardless of who selects the counsel, the counsel's clients are Indemnitees, not Indemnitor.

5.06. In addition to the indemnity required under this Contract, each Indemnitee may, at its own expense, participate in its defense by counsel of its choosing without relieving or impairing Indemnitor's obligations under this indemnity paragraph.

5.07. Indemnitor may not settle any Indemnified Claim without the consent of the City of ?????, whether or not the City is an Indemnitee as to the particular Indemnified Claim, unless (A) the settlement will be fully funded by Indemnitor and (B) the proposed settlement does not contain an admission of liability or wrongdoing by any Indemnitee. The City's withholding its consent as allowed in the preceding sentence does not release or impair Indemnitor's obligations of this indemnity paragraph. Even if the City of ????? is not an Indemnitee as to a particular Indemnified Claim, Indemnitor must give City at least 20 days advance written notice of the details of a proposed settlement before it becomes binding. Any settlement purporting to bind an Indemnitee must first be approved by City Council.

5.08. Nothing in this Contract waives governmental immunity or other defenses of Indemnitees under applicable law.

5.09. If, for whatever reason, a court refuses to enforce this indemnity as written, and only in that case, the parties must contribute to any Indemnified Claim 5% by the Indemnitees, collectively, and 95% by the Indemnitor. Indemnitor need look only to the City of ????? for Indemnitees' 5% if the City of ????? is an Indemnified Party as to a particular Indemnified Claim.

6. Termination.

6.01. City may terminate this Permission at any time before expiration by giving Joint User 120-days written notice, but only if City Council passes a resolution finding that Joint User's use of the Premises has, or in the future may reasonably be expected to, interfere with use of the Premises. City shall use good faith efforts to notify Joint User at least ten (10) days in advance of any such public meeting at which such resolution will be considered by City Council. City will consider Joint User's request for more than 120 days within which to remove and relocate its infrastructure.

6.02. Upon expiration or termination, all rights and privileges cease, and Joint User must promptly cease use of the Premises. If City terminates, City will then reimburse Joint User for the reasonable costs of (A) removing existing facilities permitted by this agreement, (B) acquiring a new location for the facilities, and (C) installing replacement facilities in the new location.

6.03. Improvements or appurtenances not removed within 90 days after termination of the Permission, whether by expiration or otherwise, become the property of City. City, may without liability to Joint User, dispose of such property at a public or private sale, without notice to Joint User.

6.04. Joint User may terminate this License at any time by abandoning its use of the Premises and delivering notice to City.

7. Assignment.
This Permission cannot be assigned by Joint User except to a certificated utility provider succeeding to Joint User's wastewater utility in the area in which the Premises are located.

8. Condemnation.
If the Premises are taken, in whole or in part, by eminent domain not for the benefit of City, then this Permission, at the option of City, ceases on the date title to the land so taken or transferred vests in the condemning authority. Joint User waives all rights

to any condemnation proceeds, unless Joint User is an agency or other part of the City. If Joint User remains an agency or other part of the City, the parties will equitably allocate the proceeds.

9. Taxes.
City is a governmental entity and does not expect to pay taxes. Joint User is responsible for taxes, if any, arising from its use of the Premises under this agreement. In no case will City ever be responsible for taxes, local, state, or federal, if any, that may be assessed against Joint User.

10. Appropriations.
All obligations of the City of ????? under this instrument are funded at the discretion of City Council. If the City Council fails to appropriate money for an obligation arising under this agreement, the City cannot be required to fulfill the obligation.

11. Dispute Resolution.
11.01. As a condition precedent to bringing any action arising out of or relating to this agreement or any aspect thereof, including an action for declaratory relief but not an action specifically excepted below, the disputants must first submit in good faith to mediation. The parties may not assert limitations, laches, waiver, and estoppel based upon attempts to mediate.

11.02. Filing suit on a claim that should be mediated hereunder waives the filer's right to demand mediation. But one party's waiver does not affect another party's right. A defendant does not waive mediation for so long as, within a reasonable time after appearing, the defendant gives written notice to the plaintiff or its counsel of intent to require compliance with this paragraph.

11.03. Mediation must be conducted in ?????????????????????

11.04. The party desiring relief has the burden to initiate mediation. Waiting for another party to initiate mediation does not waive the right to it.

11.05. If the parties can otherwise agree on a mediator, they may do so. On the other hand, either party may petition any court of competent jurisdiction to appoint a mediator. The only predicate issues the court need consider before appointing a mediator are whether (i) the copy of the contract before the court is authentic and (ii) the contract was duly signed and delivered by all parties to be bound to mediate. If neither of those issues is denied under oath, the court may appoint a mediator upon motion, without trial.

11.06. Mediator fees must be borne equally.

11.07. The parties need not mediate before going to court to seek emergency injunctive relief.

12. Miscellaneous Provisions.
12.01. **Relationship Limited.** This instrument creates only the relationship of City and Joint User. The parties are not principal and agent, partners, joint venturers, or participants in any common enterprise.

12.02. **Consent/Approval of City.** As to any matter hereunder in which City's consent is required, the consent may be granted by the Director, ?????????, as designee of the City Manager, without council action, unless the City Charter requires City Council action.

12.03. **Severability.** If any portion hereof is determined to be invalid or unenforceable, the determination does not affect the remainder hereof.

12.04. **Successors.** This Permission inures to the benefit of and binds the heirs, representatives, successors, and permitted assigns of each party. This clause does not authorize any assignment not otherwise authorized.

12.05. **Integration. This Written Permission Represents The Final Agreement Between The Parties And May Not Be Contradicted By Evidence Of Prior, Contemporaneous, Or Subsequent Oral Agreements Of The Parties. There Are No Oral Agreements Between The Parties.**

12.06. **Modification.** This Permission may not be changed orally but only by a written agreement, signed by the party against whom enforcement of any modification is sought. No such modification, express or implied, affects the right of the modifying party to require observance of either (i) any other term or (ii) the same term or condition as it applies on a subsequent or previous occasion.

12.07. **Third Party Beneficiaries.** This Permission is intended for the benefit of the parties hereto and their successors and permitted assigns only. There are no third party beneficiaries hereof.

12.08. **Notices.** Any notice provided for or permitted hereunder must be in writing and by certified mail, return receipt requested, addressed to the parties at their respective addresses set forth at the beginning. The giving of notice is complete three days after its deposit, properly addressed and postage prepaid, with the United

States Postal Service. Failure to use certified mail does not defeat the effectiveness of notice actually received, but such notice is effective only on actual receipt. Address for notice may be changed by giving notice hereunder.

12.09. **Captions.** Paragraph captions in this Permission are for ease of reference only and do not affect the interpretation hereof.

12.10. **Counterparts.** This Permission may be executed in multiple counterparts, each of which is an original, whether or not all parties sign the same document. Regardless of the number of counterparts, they constitute only one agreement. In making proof of this Permission, one need not produce or account for more counterparts than necessary to show execution by or on behalf of all parties.

12.11. **Further Assurances.** The parties must execute and deliver such additional documents and instruments as may be required to effect fully the provisions hereof. But no such additional document(s) may alter the rights or obligations of the parties as contained in this Permission.

13. Public Information.
Joint User acknowledges that this instrument is public information within the meaning of Chapter 552 of the Texas Government Code and accordingly may be disclosed to the public.

In Witness Whereof, the parties have caused their representatives to set their hands.

/signature blocks for parties/

You know, ever since I was a little girl I knew that if you look both ways when you cross the street, you'll see a lot more than traffic.

Mae West

———